SLAYING
YOUR FEAR
GIANTS

*Moving from a Jungle of Terror
to a Garden of Peace*

SLAYING YOUR FEAR GIANTS

*Moving from a Jungle of Terror
to a Garden of Peace*

CECILLE VALORIA

Published by Author Academy Elite
P.O. Box 43, Powell, OH 43035

www.AuthorAcademyElite.com

Paperback: ISBN 978-1-64085-803-9
Hardback: ISBN 978-1-64085-804-6
Ebook: ISBN 978-1-64085-805-3

Library of Congress Control Number: 2019910686

Cover design by Debbie O'Byrne
Editors- Marvin Wilmes
Jane VanVooren Rogers

*To God Almighty, Jesus Christ my Savior,
the Author and Perfecter of my faith,
and the All-Powerful Holy Spirit.*

*To Sal, Camille, Chris, and Christian,
You are my precious blessings and treasure.*

TABLE OF CONTENTS

Foreword
xiii

Prologue
xv

Part 1: Acquiring Knowledge

Chapter 1
Meet My Giant and My Jungle
3

Chapter 2
My Story
7

Chapter 3
Am I Going Nuts?
12

Part 2: Acquiring Power

Chapter 4
First Steps
21

Chapter 5
My Sling and the Power Behind It
28

Chapter 6
Growing Gardens
32

Chapter 7
A Fork in the Road
37

Chapter 8
From Garden to Jungle
43

Part 3: Acquiring Peace and Healing

Chapter 9
The First Stone—His Perfect Love
51

Chapter 10
The Second Stone—Perspective
56

Chapter 11
The Third Stone—Praise
65

Chapter 12
The Fourth Stone—Passion & Prayer
74

Chapter 13
The Fifth Stone—Perseverance
79

Part 4: Acquiring Maintenance

Chapter 14
Drought Resistant, Drought Tolerant, Drought
Avoidance
105

Epilogue
113

Acknowledgements
119

Notes
123

About the Author
129

Give thanks to the Lord, for he is good;
his love endures forever.
Let the redeemed of the Lord tell their story—
those he redeemed from the hand of the foe,
those he gathered from the lands,
from east and west, from north to south.
Psalm 107:1–3 NIV

FOREWORD

There are books that you can pick up, read several chapters, and leave a bookmark to come to it later. But this book is one that a reader would have difficulty putting down without finishing it cover to cover.

The enthralling vignettes of personal experiences, passages from the Bible, and the historical footnotes gracefully hew a story that is compelling reading for any age. It gives a glimpse of the vexing challenge in our modern society—how to conquer one's demons.

Anxiety can be an extremely debilitating condition. Coupled with traumatic experiences, it can push a person into a long illness, which if not intervened with, can have a lifelong negative effect.

This book takes the reader on a journey to instances in Cecille Valoria's life, that most times would have life-changing implications for the better or for the worse. Instead of succumbing to her fears she drew strength from within herself, her relationship with her Savior, and religious beliefs, to forge ahead and conquer her fears. A lesson to learn for many who crumble and surrender to their demons.

Cecille wrote this book telling the story of her dark side but not making herself sound like a heroine. Rather, showing in a "matter-of-fact way" how she could overcome the excruciating experiences of her life from childhood to adulthood and in such a way that it may be a help for others who might experience the same.

This is a "must-read" book.

Richard Kempis, D.D.S.
President, San Francisco Filipino Cultural Center

PROLOGUE

The microphone blared her name and announced the musical piece she would perform. She headed out to where the grand piano stood. It appeared so much heftier than the last time she had seen it just a few minutes earlier. As she neared the bench, her eyes strayed to the roomful of parents and visitors. The room's walls seemed to close in around her. The room was quiet, yet deafening. She could hear her black polished shoes moving across the solid wood floors. Tucking her shoulder-length, curly, brown hair behind her ears, she smiled at the audience and curtsied. She pushed the piano bench closer to the console so it would be easier for her feet to reach the pedals down below.

She sat and spread out the skirt of the new, white, floral-embroidered dress her parents bought her for this occasion. Back straight, just the way her teacher taught her, her posture was a "go." She laid her ten little fingers in the required arched position on top of the black-and-white keys. She had waited with excitement for months for this moment to showcase her music. And here it was.

Her cold fingers shook as she played. The notes did not come out the way she wanted them to. Her musical piece's tempo, an adagio, flew faster than the ticking metronome. An allegro reverberated the rhythm of her heart like the rapid movement of a cheetah in pursuit of its prey. The piano piece was right in front of her. She had a cheat sheet in place, just in case. But her eyes did not work. The musical composition she had practiced, played, and memorized for months before this day was no longer available for her easy access. Elusive. Her mind languished under clouds that obscured her vision. She played the limited parts she recalled, but her fingers were stiff and did not cooperate. She wanted to strike the "A" note, but she tapped the "B." The melody did not sound right—a failure. Skipped stanzas and off-beat notes dominated, but she persevered to the ending. It was sheer torture for this eight-year-old girl. Though ready to burst into tears, she contained her feelings. It was time to face the crowd and bow. The crowd clapped, but to her it sounded like "boos."

Turning from the spectators, she slipped away to the back of the stage, tears streaming down her face.

That girl was me.

Part 1

Acquiring Knowledge

"Knowledge and power are synonymous."

—Francis Bacon

CHAPTER 1

Meet My Giant and My Jungle

With the valley between them, the Philistine army positioned themselves occupying one hill and the Israelites the other. They drew their battle lines. While the Israelite soldiers waited for the fight to start, David approached them to deliver food and supplies to his brothers. Nearing the battlefield, he saw and heard Goliath shouting to the soldiers, "Why do you come out and line up for battle? Am I not a Philistine, and are you not the servants of Saul? Choose a man and have him come down to me. If he is able to fight and kill me, we will become your subjects; but if I overcome him and kill him, you will become our subjects and serve us."

Goliath continued, "This day I defy the armies of Israel! Give me a man and let us fight each other."

Saul and his soldiers were terrified.

"Who is this uncircumcised Philistine that he should defy the armies of the living God?" David asked the soldiers. (1 Samuel 17: 8–11).

David knew the right question to ask. Knowing our enemy is crucial.

If you have read *The Godfather* series or seen its movies, you might recall Michael Corleone alluding to this.

"My dad taught me numerous things here—he educated me in this room. He trained me—hold your friends close but your enemies closer."[1]

Sun-Tzu, a Chinese military strategist had the same line of thinking when he said, "Know your enemy and know yourself and you will always be victorious."[2] It alludes the idea that knowing who you are fighting against will enable you to win your battle.

We will come up with effective strategies against our enemy, intimidator, or a challenge if we know who or what is opposing us. I had to identify mine. Let me introduce you to my giant and my jungle.

My Giant

Several weeks had passed since the rattling piano recital. With Christmas and New Year celebrations over, it was time to go back to school. I was eager to return but felt uneasy. *What if my friends laugh at me, don't like me anymore, or think I'm weird?*

After the disastrous performance, I believed something was wrong with me. *Why were my other classmates able to perform their music well and I was not? Was I just bad? Did they feel the same way I did? Were they scared like I was?*

I experienced similar symptoms on several different occasions. I encountered them during performances. Then I felt them when I had class presentations. I suffered from frequent stomach aches. People wondered if I ate too much or ate too little. Was there something else going on inside my tiny abdomen? I visited the emergency room often. Face-to-face visits with ER doctors, hearing the beeping noises, and being aware of the bustling activity in the emergency room did not help. Like a hound with its tail tucked between its legs, I became even more apprehensive. My heart raced, my hands got colder, my breathing grew labored. I experienced emotions and feelings I couldn't understand or shake.

During one of those occasions, I overheard the doctor say, "This girl will have a CVA (cardiovascular accident)." I didn't know what that meant, but I reckoned it was something serious. After hearing his comment, my mind played an endless melody of fabricated tales. *Something is wrong with me. I am dying. I am crazy.*

The ER physician gave it a name: Generalized anxiety disorder (GAD). He identified my giant! I was tagged.

He prescribed Valium, an anxiolytic. Even at a low dose, it calmed me. I saw its value. It made me sad to realize that while other kids my age were carefree and bold, I was at the mercy of a pill to help me deal with my worries. It kept me functioning.

My Jungle

Fear dwarfs, blinds, mutes, and deafens us. Walking through a jungle does the same. From the book, "In Search of the Rainforest," Wikipedia noted, "The word 'jungle' itself carries connotations of untamed and uncontrollable nature and isolation from civilisation, along with the emotions that evokes: threat, confusion, powerlessness, disorientation and immobilisation."[3]

These words described my emotions to a T. I had an array of feelings that without warning, could rise to unimaginable proportions. Once my anxiety symptoms started, they escalated. The nightmare I had during my piano recital days pops up, consuming me with fear.

I worried constantly even when there was no specific threat. My active mind went from thoughts of "I'm sick" to "I'm dying." I always thought the worst-case scenario about everything. My racing thoughts led to an increased heart rate, and my hands got cold, clammy, shaking, and stiff; I was unable to think, talk well, and move with ease. My stomach turned into knots. I wandered through my jungle more and more. I got carried away to this place of tangled vegetation, an overgrown forest, with my wrists tied behind my back, leaving me defenseless to whatever lurked above, below, and all around.

CHAPTER 2

My Story

My teacher in elementary "killed two birds with one stone" by teaching our class aphorisms in our native dialect to target both the study of our national language and our cultural beliefs. One saying I learned in my vernacular was, *"Ang taong hindi lilingon sa pinangalingan ay hindi makakarating sa patutunguhan."* In English this says, "A person who does not look back at where he came from will not get to where he is going." Looking back at our past would enable us to have compassion and empathy for those who are going through the same things we did. So let me take you back to my humble beginnings.

The year was 1960. It was a year of many firsts around the world. The *Flintstones* cartoon premiered, and a presidential debate was aired for the first time on television. Cassius Clay (Muhammed Ali) won his first professional fight in Louisville, Kentucky. Aluminum cans were introduced. It was the year when France first tested their atomic bomb. The United States launched the world's first nuclear-powered aircraft carrier, the USS Enterprise, and the first weather satellite, TIROS-1. New inventions included the laser, the pacemaker, and the first commercial copier.[4]

While all this was happening around the world, on a quiet Monday in September, in a charming city on a peninsula at the heart of the Pacific Ocean, I was born. My dad's sister nicknamed me Tinette, because I had a small appetite and was a tiny baby. They christened me, their long-awaited girl, Cilie Ann, a combination of my parent's names, Cecilia and Antonio. I remained Cilie Ann until I was old enough to say I disliked that name.

"*Sili*" pronounced like my first name, Cilie, meant "pepper" in our dialect. Putting my given and middle name together, Cilie Ann sounded like "*Sili-an*" which implied "to apply pepper." To curtail us kids from cussing, our elders would say, "*Sili-an nako imong babá*," meaning, "I will put pepper in your mouth." I feared my name would be a source of teasing, and I could not handle that. Combined with all the other issues I had, I so disliked it I asked my parents to change my name. Understanding my concerns, they renamed me Cecille Ann.

My parents lavished my brothers and me with love. They were kind, devout in their faith, but strict. We attended church services every Wednesday and Sunday. The church was a place both of solace and fear. The moral standards and rules we had to adhere to were rigid. I feared going to confession, concerned the priest might tell me how bad I was. I did not have the comfort of knowing the Lord for myself because I heard only priests could touch and read the Bible. All I learned about the Lord was through what I was told. My responsibility was to attend Mass, listen to adults, follow, and obey. Kids were to be seen, not heard. During meals, our parents expected us to eat, not be a part of the adult conversation. They instructed us to listen and be obedient to our elders.

Daddy was from Luzon, the biggest island in the northern part of the Philippine Archipelago. We lived two days and a night away by boat from this main island. Every summer, Mommy and I would take a trip to visit my cousins and other relatives on my dad's side. These were times when I could not get to sleep. My anxiety developed to its height while onboard the ship. The smell of diesel permeated the hallways in the ship and made me want to throw up.

As our ship rocked from the huge waves in the vast open ocean, my mind filled itself up with images of the vessel capsizing, sinking, or getting stranded somewhere. Memories of previous times when our ship had to seek safe refuge at the closest harbor while we waited for unexpected storms to pass, crept back. Or the time we got stranded because we strayed into shallow waters and a fisherman's net got tangled with the propeller of the boat, though wide awake, these were my nightmares. My mom had Valium ready for such times as these.

Both well-educated, Mommy was a nurse and Daddy an engineer. Our family was in the upper-middle-class, so we had the privilege of having a helper, a nanny, and a chauffeur. My parents concentrated on their careers. They did not have to concern themselves with the routine management of our household.

The age gap between each of us siblings was three years. Being an only girl and the youngest, I felt lonely and regarded myself powerless compared to my older brothers. They were closer to each other. I hung out more with my nannies. My nannies offered the companionship I needed but spending most of my afternoons with them was not all that healthy.

Though the antennas mounted on our roofs were tall, shows played on our television were fleeting and boringly black and white. The radio was the mainstay. Stories of beheaded priests, beasts, and *manananggals* aired on the radio programs every afternoon exercising our creative imagery and fantasies. They aired about the same time we had to take our siesta. A nap was a ritual and a must for all growing children. According to the old folks, if we didn't do this it would stunt our growth (hmm, maybe there was truth to this, as I remained short).

Manananggals were witches who could detach their torsos and take off like bats. They sought pregnant women and would fly to their rooftops at night. Their strong, elongated tongues pierced through thatched roofs to reach the bellies of these mothers and suck the blood and heart out of the fetus. The word "manananggal" is a common parlance that meant "to separate or take away."

These stories were common myths that added fuel to my already fertile and unbridled imagination. As my nanny listened to the stories on the radio during my nap times, I suffered the collateral damage since I heard the stories, too. I developed a fear of the dark and of being alone.

Superstitious beliefs were predominant and influenced our way of living. Our forefathers believed supernatural beings (dwarves, fairies, ghouls, goblins) inhabited nature and other things around us. They taught us to say, "Excuse me" while walking by trees or anthills because we might step on one of those characters and irritate them. They told us not to sweep at night because if we did, we would sweep wealth away. A young lady shouldn't sing while cooking as this will cause her to be an old maid. If you are a bride-to-be, trying on your gown before your wedding, would cost you your life. These were just a few of the superstitions they raised me with that were not conducive to a peaceful existence.

Did my upbringing lead to my propensity to develop anxiety? There has always been a debate on whether nature or nurture caused disease and health challenges. Researchers are baffled by the causes of distress and fears, but they have identified a person's genes and environment as factors. Would looking into these even make a difference?

I don't know what your story is, but I know that each one of us has a remarkable story to tell. I believe the experiences we had or have, play an essential part in our fears and anxiety. The past we grew up with influences who we are today. Understanding this allows us to have empathy for each other.

Does it help to go back, unearth, or ruminate on our past? I would say, it depends on the situation. Where are you in your journey? Have you taken your first steps, and if you have, how can you best move forward? You know yourself better than anyone else.

I decided not to get stuck in my past. I will look back on it to keep me humble and more sensitive to others going through the same challenges, but otherwise, I would rather leave it behind, move forward, and heal. What about you?

CHAPTER 3

Am I Going Nuts?

Having been a long-time Windows PC user, switching to Mac proved to be a challenging feat. My rudimentary skills became more apparent when I started having problems with my computer, wireless mouse, and keyboard. For days, the Apple technicians had to contend with multiple questions from this newbie. With their guidance, I performed several technological maneuvers to re-establish the link between the Bluetooth on my iMac and my keyboard and mouse.

The first part of the diagnostic process was to make sure my desktop was in good working order. I powered it off and then back on. That component earned a check mark. It was time to examine the other parts. I powered off my keyboard as directed, then using a cable hooked it to my iMac. As soon as I connected it, I switched my keyboard on, then disconnected it from my computer after a few seconds. This action allowed the Bluetooth on my computer to recognize and connect to my keyboard's Bluetooth. I followed the same procedure for the mouse. To my delight, it worked!

Our brain is like a computer. Both of their parts and functions parallel each other. Communication, power supply, and systems are common parlances that apply to both. Resembling a computer, the different parts of our brain work interrelatedly. These parts work together and function as a system. Just like my keyboard, computer, and mouse, optimum communication between each component is necessary for all of them to perform their job well.

I used to get upset when people told me, "It's all in your head," when they saw the external symptoms of my fears. People who had no clue what I was going through had this reaction. On the outside, I appeared healthy, like everyone else. They were oblivious of the turmoil boiling inside me. This comment did not help when I questioned my sanity. Although I did not confront them, I would walk away sulking. *It's not just in my head! It's not only in my head!*

But what if I said there is some truth to their statement?

Let me explain.

Physiological Basis of Anxiety

Our body is made of different types of cells (muscle, nerve, epithelial or skin cells). A collection of similar cells form tissues (muscular tissue, nervous tissue, epithelial tissue) that perform a specific job. The tissues work together to form organs (stomach, heart, lungs). Organs work hand in hand to become systems (cardiac, respiratory, urinary, lymphatic, limbic, etc.). Each system has a specific responsibility. Collectedly, the systems work to enable our body to perform all bodily functions (breathing, walking, running, thinking) like a well-oiled machine.

The limbic system which is positioned above the brain stem and spinal cord is responsible for emotions, survival instincts, and memory.[5] Multiple parts of the brain—the amygdala, the hippocampus, hypothalamus, thalamus, each contribute their unique function to form the limbic system.

To understand the pathophysiology behind anxiety, let's break down the different parts of the limbic system and the autonomic nervous system by outlining their functions and then interrelating them.

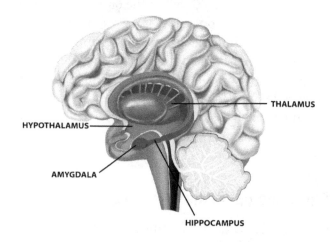

THALAMUS

HYPOTHALAMUS

AMYGDALA

HIPPOCAMPUS

Thalamus

Except for the sense of smell, our nerves relay the sensations we experience (sight, touch, taste, and hear) to the thalamus.[6] As the thalamus sends these nerve impulses to various parts of the brain, it stimulates those parts to act or react.

The Hippocampus

The part of the limbic system that converts short-term memory to long-term memory is the hippocampus. Memory plays an essential role in our emotions.

The Hypothalamus

The hypothalamus regulate the autonomic nervous system (ANS) and other basic drives. The ANS is made up of two different branches—the sympathetic nervous system (SNS) and the parasympathetic nervous system (PNS). These two have different functions and effects.

When immediate danger or stressful situations confront us (i.e., we see someone lurking in the dark and think, *he is after me*), the sympathetic nervous system kicks into gear, giving our body the means to fight or flight. Our body, either stays in place to challenge our aggressors, freezes, or runs away from them. When we feel we are in danger, the SNS causes our adrenal glands to release hormones called adrenaline (epinephrine) and cortisol into our blood stream. These hormones cause the subsequent changes in our body—increased heart rate, dilated pupils, increased respiration, decreased salivation, and an increase in glucose and oxygen—aimed at helping us fight or run.[7]

As we become anxious and have irrational thoughts, stress, and constant worry (even in the absence of real threats), high levels of adrenaline and cortisol remain in our bloodstream.[8] This keeps us continually on edge. Prolonged high levels of these hormones are detrimental to our heart and other vital organs. This knowledge made me understand why the doctor said that I might develop a CVA.

The parasympathetic nervous system produces the opposite effect—the "rest and digest" response. When stimulated, the PNS releases the hormone acetylcholine. The release of this hormone causes our heart rate to go down, decreases glucose available to our body, constricts our pupils, and decreases our respiration.[9]

Amygdala

Ironically, the part of the limbic system that is primarily responsible for anxiety, fear, and aggression is a pair of almond-shaped bundles of nerves in the middle of the brain. These bundles sit one on each hemisphere, thus, a right and left amygdala. Conclusions on the role of the amygdala have resulted from studies on people who have injured this part of their brain. Researchers found that patients whose amygdalae were stimulated became more aggressive, or violent, or they became more fearful and anxious. Those who had severed amygdalae exhibited fewer inhibitions, became calmer, and felt less fearful.[10]

Many researchers explain the connection between the parts of the limbic system in terms of conditioning. Taking the example above of the man lurking in the shadows, our observation of perceived danger is transmitted by nerve pathways to our thalamus. The thalamus relays this perception to the amygdala, the hippocampus, and hypothalamus. If we experienced this same scenario before, and it resulted in our lives being threatened, then we react in fear. This fear reaction triggers our hypothalamus to activate the SNS, and our bodies are prepared to either fight, flight, or freeze. Memories of varying experiences evoke different emotions.

So, when people say, "it's all in your head," I would agree there is some truth to it. Like the CPU of a computer, our brains process the thoughts we have, our memories, and perception of impulses. It's still not "*all* in our heads." We don't just imagine our symptoms. They are real and affect our entire body and well-being.

Am I nuts because I have anxiety?

I can confidently say, "No!"

Part 2

Acquiring Power

"Power is about self-preservation; principle focuses on making ideas successful."

—Dan Webster

CHAPTER 4

First Steps

Anxiety took hold of me throughout my elementary and high school years. The symptoms were there—the nerves, shaking hands, marathon heart rate, stomach aches—but they did not stop me from getting involved in activities. I don't know if it was just that I got used to them, or that I was hard-nosed. As Georgia O'Keeffe, a great American artist of the 20th-century and dubbed the "Mother of American Modernism"[11] once said, "I've been absolutely terrified every moment of my life, and I've never let it keep me from doing a single thing I wanted to do,"[12] I did the same. I had the gift of being able to carry a tune, and I loved singing. When I was in third grade, a year after my diagnosis, I entered a neighborhood singing competition, twice. I sang and trembled my way to garner second place, both times. *Come to think of it; I might have won first place had I not had to restart singing each time!*

Even at a young age, I learned to accept my symptoms. I determined they might discourage me, but they will not diminish me.

In sixth grade, I auditioned for a part in our school choir and got accepted. "The Young Singers," as they called us, competed in the local, then regional level and won. We advanced to the national level and took home the first-place trophy. We did this two years in a row!

The victories provided us with the opportunity to meet our president, Ferdinand Marcos, and his First Lady, Imelda Marcos. We performed for them in the privacy of the beautiful Malacañang Palace. The First Lady serenaded us back with a superb rendition of "Matud Nila," one of the popular Visayan songs that hailed from the island and province where she was born. They even treated us to a tour of a museum that held all her used dresses and shoes. That was such an exciting addition to our win!

The elementary school I attended was part of a prominent private school started by American missionaries. For a week every August, we had varying activities around the large university to celebrate its founding. These involved the elementary, high school, and the colleges. In my primary years, each grade level would prepare either a song, a skit, or a dance. These were all anxiety-producing events for me.

We held our performances on the stage in front of the basketball courts. We took our chairs out and positioned them close to the stage, while the custodian lined up chairs in rows behind us for parents and guests. Being the shortest did not help, because I was always in the front row when we performed. However, my confidence increased because I had my classmates dancing or singing beside me, and I was not performing all by myself. It was not as threatening, but I still felt my hands getting clammy and shaky, and my heart pounding.

When I got to high school, our part of the celebration was to learn and perform folk dances. Our physical education teachers taught and prepared us months in advance for this big production. We danced in a big open field next to our university library, cultural center, and gym. Though exciting, again these were nerve-wracking days for me.

• • •

A Chinese philosopher Lao Tzu said, "a journey of a thousand miles begins with a single step."[13] Likewise, David in 1 Samuel 17:32 assured Saul, "…your servant will go and fight with him." David did not retreat. He took a step toward the intimidating giant.

Nothing can be achieved without the deed.

When action is absent, achievement will not be present.

Toward the end of my senior year in high school, I took the first step in my battle against my Fear Giant and the jungle in which it enclosed me.

I was invited to a Campus Crusade for Christ meeting where I met several missionaries for CCC. Two

> **Nothing can be achieved without the deed. When action is absent, achievement will not be present.**

of them were Dan and Cory Varela, a young, married couple who served together. Kuya Dan ("ku-ya," a term for brotherly respect) was the Director for our region. Ate Cory ("A-té," a term to call a woman older than you), as we young ladies affectionately and respectfully called her, led the women's ministry.

Campus Crusade for Christ uses the Four Spiritual Laws tract to help explain the laws behind the relationship between God and man. It talks about how we (human beings) are sinners. Our sinfulness separated us from our Holy God. When Jesus Christ came down to Earth and was crucified as an atonement for our sins, God restored the bridge that would enable us to have access to Him again. Our part is to acknowledge our sinfulness, repent, and accept Jesus Christ's sacrifice. We must surrender our lives to Him and ask Him to be our Savior and Lord. This act of faith is our acknowledgment we need a savior.

> **When Jesus Christ came down to Earth and was crucified as an atonement for our sins, God restored the bridge that would enable us to have access to Him again.**

An internationally recognized symbol in battle is the white flag. It symbolizes surrender, asking for protection and a truce—recognition that combatants cannot save themselves. It assures them of a ceasefire and freedom from being killed.

Ate Cory shared the Four Spiritual Laws with me. That same day, I accepted Jesus Christ and surrendered my life to Him. I waved the white flag, acknowledging my need for His peace and protection. I recognized the fact that I could not fight my battles on my own. I surrendered my life to the One who could.

David asked Saul's permission to fight Goliath. Saul hesitated because of David's youth. We all have something inside us that makes us feel inferior and smaller than what we face—be it our youth, timidity, or our lack of skills, education, strength, or power. When we go through anxiety, we see a force bigger than us. The enormity of irrational thoughts, unstoppable worry, and fears confront us—foremost being the fear of death and dying. We see ourselves as helpless amid an overpowering giant. Rationality flows out the door and it leaves us with trembling, torture, and confusion.

David could have given himself over to the same insecurities that the Israelites held, but he remembered the lessons he learned while tending his father's sheep. In boldness he proclaimed, "The Lord who rescued me from the paw of the lion and the paw of the bear will rescue me from the hand of this Philistine" (1 Samuel 17:37). His confidence was not in himself but in His God, who had been his protector.

As David faced Goliath and heard his taunting, he continued, "All those gathered here will know that it is not by sword or spear that the Lord saves; for the battle is the Lord's, and He will give all of you into our hands" (1 Samuel 17:47).

David knew he could depend on the Lord as He had proven Himself faithful to him in the daily circumstances of his life.

It was easy for me to see that this was what I was missing in my young life. I finally owned my relationship with the Lord, and not just that which was automatically handed down to me by my parents. Don't get me wrong. The discipline, love, and faith my parents modeled paved the way for me. Without knowing it, this faith and love gave me the courage to sing while trembling during those competitions. My parents' love and faith helped me stand in front of the class when I had to recite things or raise my hand to answer. It was the faith and love they had for me that allowed me to control the symptoms when I had a task to complete. When we don't have what it takes to get us through our challenges, we latch on to the strength, faith, and hope other people around us have to carry us through our tough times.

I had my parents' love and faith. These helped me through my difficulties, but I needed to connect with God. I needed to see His power, faithfulness, and manifestation for myself.

When I accepted Jesus as my Lord and Savior, a sense of peace enveloped my heart. I finally found Someone I could hold on to when fear engulfed me. Someone who held me tightly when I couldn't see, hear, or feel the truths that my mind twisted. Someone who would fight my giant for me. Someone who would take a weed whacker and clear my jungle. All I needed to do was keep my eyes on Him and stand firm as He took me by my hand.

The story of King Jehoshaphat leading the people of Judah to the Desert of Tekoa to prepare against the invasion of the Moabites, Meunites, and Ammonites illustrates this truth. King Jehoshaphat knew they were preparing to fight against a huge army. Not knowing what to do, he prayed for help from the Lord. The Spirit of the Lord spoke to them through a Levite, Jahaziel, saying, "Don't be afraid or discouraged because of this large army. The battle is not your battle, it is God's. Tomorrow go down there and fight those people. They will come up through the Pass of Ziz. You will find them at the end of the ravine that leads to the Desert of Jeruel. You won't need to fight in this battle. Just stand strong in your places, and you will see the Lord save you. Judah and Jerusalem, don't be afraid or discouraged, because the Lord is with you. So go out against those people tomorrow" (2 Chronicles 20:15–17).

My journey toward finding my garden of peace started with Him—the only true source of peace and healing. My first step led me toward the Cross, not away from it. I had to start at the foot of the Cross. Without this first step, all the strategies and techniques I used would have fallen short.

CHAPTER 5

My Sling and the Power Behind It

Saul knew David needed protection to fight Goliath. He offered him what he had—his own armor. David was not used to the ensemble, but he was familiar with his own—a sling and stones. He refused Saul's armor. Instead he readied his sling and picked up five stones from the Brook Elah.[14]

Goliath moved closer. He said to David, "'Am I a dog, that you come at me with sticks?' And the Philistine cursed David by his gods. 'Come here,' he said, 'and I'll give your flesh to the birds and the wild animals!'" (1 Samuel 17).

Confident of his God, David replied, "You come against me with sword and spear and javelin, but I come against you in the name of the Lord Almighty, the God of the armies of Israel, whom you have defied. This day the Lord will deliver you into my hands, and I'll strike you down and cut off your head. This very day I will give the carcasses of the Philistine army to the birds and the wild animals, and the whole world will know that there is a God in Israel. All those gathered here will know that it is not by sword or spear that the Lord saves; for the battle is the Lord's, and he will give all of you into our hands " (1 Samuel 17:45–47). And he dashed to the battle line, took a stone from his pouch, hoisting it from his sling straight into Goliath's forehead, slaying him.

When I first heard this story, I pictured a modern Y-shaped slingshot. On further research, I discovered that in Biblical times the slings they had was not attached to a stick. They were made of leather and woven plant material. Those who used these weapons were called slingers.[15] They swung them to release whatever projectile they used as a missile. Their power came from the slinger's strength. When not in use, a sling is inert but has both potential and kinetic energy available to it.

With my surrender, the Lord gave me the gift of His Holy Spirit as a guarantee of my salvation. Ephesians 1:13–14 states, "In Him, you also, after listening to the message of truth, the gospel of your salvation—having also believed, you were sealed in Him with the Holy Spirit of promise, who is given

The knowledge of the Holy Spirit's presence is important for us because the things that occupy our mind when we go through anxiety are unfounded lies.

as a pledge of our inheritance, with a view to the redemption of God's own possession, to the praise of His glory."

John 14:15–17 shows the same promise Jesus gave to His disciples before he was crucified, "If you love me, keep my commands. And I will ask the Father, and he will give you another advocate to help you and be with you forever— the Spirit of truth. The world cannot accept him, because it neither sees him nor knows him. But you know Him, for He lives with you and will be in you." He continues to say in John 14:26, "But the Advocate, the Holy Spirit, whom the Father will send in my name, will teach you all things and will remind you of everything I have said to you."

The knowledge of the Holy Spirit's presence is important for us because the things that occupy our mind when we go through anxiety are unfounded lies.

Not only does the Holy Spirit assure us of the Lord's promise of salvation, the Holy Spirit is also the Spirit of truth and power. Romans 8:11 tells us, "But if the Spirit of Him who raised Jesus from the dead dwells in you, He who raised Christ Jesus from the dead will also give life to your mortal bodies through His Spirit who dwells in you."

The apostle Paul knew where our power emanated from as he wrote in Romans 15:13, "May the God of hope fill you with all joy and peace as you trust in Him, so that you may overflow with hope by the power of the Holy Spirit."

The Holy Spirit is our source of power, life, and truth. He gives us discernment, guidance, and strength. When we take a step and use whatever God has given us—His Holy Spirit, the ability to think, make choices, decide, and act, we can achieve something. God provides us that power.

The Holy Spirit is the power behind my sling.

Not only is the Word of God "a lamp unto my feet, and a light unto my path" (Psalm 119:105) that takes the darkness and gloom when I am anxious, but it is my sling, "For the word of God is alive and active.

Sharper than any double-edged sword, it penetrates even to dividing soul and spirit, joints and marrow; it judges the thoughts and attitudes of the heart" (Hebrews 4:12).

After I accepted the Lord on May 17, 1977, miraculously, I did not need the Valium pills. Instead, I held onto my Savior, the Holy Spirit, and God's Word.

CHAPTER 6

Growing Gardens

People used to depend on the heavenly bodies to guide their activities. By looking at the pattern of the sun and the stars, they knew when to plant, harvest, store their grains, and hunt. Growing a garden follows a pattern, too. You prepare the soil, plant, tend it, and then you reap the rewards of your hard work with the beautiful flowers that bloom or the crops you produce.

My newfound faith helped me through my college years. Like growing a garden, I nourished it by surrounding myself with people who were seeking to grow in their relationship with the Lord. Campus Crusade for Christ was an active part of my life. I discipled young ladies, which not only grew their faith but also mine. I found and memorized Scripture verses to cling to when the jungle was reappearing and would encroach. "I can do all this through Him who gives me strength" (Philippians 4:13) and "Do not be anxious about anything, but in every situation, by prayer and petition, with thanksgiving, present your requests to God. And the peace of God, which transcends all understanding, will guard your hearts and your minds in Christ Jesus" (Philippians 4:6–7) became my lifelines. These passages helped me focus on Jesus Christ, who was greater than my Fear Giant and could slay him. I had Him who was fighting for me and with me. This knowledge brought me peace. Though the occasional fluttering in my heart still cropped up, I held on to my scriptural lifelines, my sling. Anxiety did not faze me.

I took a public speaking class as one of my electives. It was nerve-wracking, but I presented a speech on "How to Create an Ikebana Flower Arrangement" for my final project. With my hands shaking and my heart beating faster than usual, I showed twenty classmates and my professor how to arrange flowers to symbolize heaven, man, and earth.

I became involved in performing. I acted in several productions like *The Man of La Mancha*, *Tinimbang Ka Ngunit Kulang* (*You Were Weighed but You Were Lacking*), and other plays in my native language. My courage in college was strong.

My confidence in the Lord and His faithfulness did not stop there. I applied for and made it into medical school. Given that I previously trembled at the sight of white walls and uniformed men and women, cringed at the beeping sounds of the cardiac monitors, and hated the smell of Lysol-scented emergency rooms, this was miraculous.

• • •

June 1981, I boarded a ship to Cebu, an island across from Dumaguete, my birthplace, to start the next chapter of my life. My parents could not believe the direction my life was taking. They knew that the mere sight of blood made me woozy.

Medical school was demanding and rigorous. Our upper classmen labeled some professors as "terrors." One might think this would add to my stress, but somehow, they did not intimidate me. The tenacity I had when I was younger and the faith I possessed helped me see them as a challenge to conquer.

Junior and senior internship years were very stressful. I rarely slept, especially when on duty. Paging codes were constantly going off signaling various kinds of emergencies. How could anyone sleep through that? I can now laugh at one particular twenty-four duty that put me in a mortifying moment.

It happened in the middle of the night. The overhead issued a Code 99 that signified a cardiopulmonary arrest. The location was the Emergency room. I remember I was just starting to doze off. On cue, I got up and dashed to the ER. I got there in no time at all, but when I looked down, to my embarrassment, I found I was only wearing my slip and blouse. I guess I'd taken off my skirt before I went to bed. Luckily, I was still adequately covered.

Helping my surgery resident friend suture the gaping wound on a patient's forehead, I found myself in another quirky moment. My job was to wipe off the oozing blood from the laceration. We were in the middle of the procedure when I felt a cold sweat on my forehead and sudden lightheadedness. My surroundings were dimming.

"I think I might faint," I whispered.

"Scrub out," was my friend's prompt response.

I took off my scrubs and retreated to a back room where I laid for a few minutes to regain my composure.

During our senior year, they assigned our clinical rotations. Obstetrics and Gynecology was one which doubled my anxiety. Delivering babies was tricky. Coming out from the birth canal, they are slimy and could slip through one's hands, which worried me a lot. I did not want to drop the newborn into the bucket below. Besides fearing I would hurt them, I knew this would end my career. Our medical preceptor forewarned us. After delivering several babies without mishap, I completed my obstetrics rotation, nullifying my fears. I moved on to the next assignment.

• • •

I made sure I lived a balanced life—I attended CCC meetings and continued discipling others. I spent weekends relaxing with friends. My roommate and I made use of our downtime by dining out, going to the movies, relaxing, and watching romantic films.

I was an excellent note-taker and had very legible penmanship. It was far from the "chicken-scratch" handwriting that was a common joke about the way physicians wrote. My classmates often borrowed my custom-bound notebooks of plain, white office paper. Very popular with them, my notebooks were out even the night before major exams. I was an early riser, and my study times from 2:00-4:00 a.m. worked well for me.

I graduated from medical school and proceeded on to my Post-Graduate Internship (PGI). Three months into my internship, I got a notice from the United

States Embassy. I was to appear for an interview in Manila so they could either approve or disapprove my long-standing visa application. Back then, when the United States Embassy called you for an interview, you did not make them wait. Things moved fast. I left with my brother for Manila and interviewed at the Consulate. An hour later, we received our visas. My brother and I completed our required physical exams, and I filed for a leave of absence from the hospital where I was working. The next month, we left for America.

CHAPTER 7

A Fork in the Road

June 1986. My twenty-nine-year-old brother and I stepped onto the plane, our conduit to this new land for which we had been waiting a long time. During my growing-up years, I heard buzz phrases like America was the "land of opportunity." People wanted to come to America. They considered us lucky to have gotten our visas.

I was excited to see my parents, who had been long-time residents of the U.S., but sad to leave behind the familiar, and everything I had worked for career-wise. Anxious thoughts plagued my mind as I dreaded the long trip. The first leg of our travel took us to Japan, a lengthy four-and-a half-hour journey over the Pacific Ocean. Since inter-island flights were an hour-and-a half to two hours long, this was the first long flight I had experienced. As the plane took off, I braced myself, clinging to the arms of my chair, akin to hanging onto a precipice for dear life. Thoughts of the plane crashing intensified as turbulence after turbulence brought our plane to abrupt changes in flying levels. My heart dropped with the sudden descents and lifted with the swift ascents.

I prayed.

Cocooned inside our plane as we embarked on the second leg of the journey, an even lengthier, eleven hours, I became restless. I preoccupied myself with the movie choice playing on the big screen in front of me and even managed a few minutes of shuteye. God gave me a visual of His hand holding our plane, which calmed me. I knew that whether our plane went up or down, it was cradled in the palm of His hand.

After what seemed an eternity, we stepped out of the airplane at the San Francisco International Airport and into what appeared to be a whole new world.

The walk from the jetway to the concourse, endless. It intensified the ambivalence I felt. I reminded myself that I could always go back to Dumaguete. I was twenty-six years old, an adult, and could make my own decisions. My parents petitioned my brother and me so we could all be together. Before my dad immigrated to the U.S., my mom could only visit us in the Philippines once a year because it was costly. Although my dad stayed with us, it was hard without my mother guiding me daily through my teen-to-young-adult years. I needed a female role model. I missed being able to talk to her after school when I had some exciting news or wasn't feeling well. During those times, long-distance communication overseas was not only costly and inconvenient but very unreliable. Calling from our house was nearly impossible. We had to go to a local phone company and wait between thirty minutes to an hour just to get the elusive, clear connection instead of the crackling and hissing static interference. With sweat rolling down our foreheads and back, we had to shout inside the stuffy, insulated cubicle so the person on the other end of the line could hear us.

Coming to America would bring our family together and open doors for us for a brighter future. That was what I tried to tell myself.

• • •

Our best laid plans sometimes do not work the way we envision them. I had planned to return to the Philippines and complete my PGI. However, going back to the Philippines was not an immediate option. Instead I worked at the San Joaquin General Hospital in Stockton as an Intensive Care Unit (ICU) clerk to keep myself connected to the medical field.

A curveball came my way the minute I met this lean, tan-skinned man in a funky pair of printed multi-colored pants and a dark shirt. He had distinctive mullet-styled hair. My aunt, Charito, introduced me to Sal.

And love beckoned.

He lived in Clovis—a two-hour drive from Stockton, where I lived with my family. During those early months of long-distance dating, we looked forward to our nine p.m. calls after we each listened to James Dobson's radio program. What he talked about became our discussion topic for that night. This cemented our spiritual connection.

The thought of returning to the Philippines became difficult, but when the opportunity presented itself, I went back to continue my PGI.

After three months, I knew I did not enjoy being even farther away from Sal. Though the pull of my career was strong, love's pull proved stronger. I came back to the U.S., six months short of completing my Post-Graduate Internship.

Love was the game-changer.

I tried to keep my career alive when I got back. Without preparing for it, I took the Medical Board Licensure exams cold turkey and failed it by six-and-a-half percent. I vowed never to retake the exam again without adequate preparation. My medical career stalled.

Sal's and my love blossomed, then took a tumultuous turn. The long distance took its toll. After less than a year, we separated ways and lost touch for years.

• • •

I enrolled at the University of the Pacific (UOP) to pursue a master's degree in behavioral medicine, a band-aid to ease the sadness of my breakup and keep me in the medical field. The decision proved to reawaken the dozing Fear Giant as I dealt with people who had anxiety and panic attack issues. Again, I had to confront my own struggles. As I helped my clients, I also learned how to use biofeedback to inform myself of how I reacted to situations and to control my breathing and heart rate.

At UOP I again got involved with Campus Crusade for Christ. This involvement led me to one of my most unforgettable adventures. I went on a one-and-a-half-month mission trip to Argentina and Bolivia with college students from around the United States. I wanted to go to Uganda but did not meet my fundraising goal. A month before the trip, they gave me a choice of other venues. I chose the South American countries over the inner-city New York mission. Travel papers had to be filled out in a very short time frame. The last-minute change threw me into an anxiety loop. The day before our trip, I flew with the group to Miami still without my visa. It was a nail-biter move. Miraculously, I got my visa from the Argentinian Embassy in Miami just an hour before our scheduled departure. The trip stretched my faith. For someone who has anxiety, this was a bold step. I did not know anyone I was traveling with, and I had to interact in a language that I could understand better than speak. But God was faithful. Though all of us students started as strangers, our Christian faith united us, and we ended up not only as brothers and sisters in Christ but also as friends. Sharing the gospel and serving others kept me from thinking of my fears and worries, and I had a blast. God also used my medical knowledge to help my group overcome altitude sickness.

A month after I got back from my trip, I held an appreciation dinner for my financial supporters.

Sal was in attendance.

We reconciled, became more serious, and got married within a short period of time.

Not only did my marital status change, so did my career. Tita Char, who was a special education teacher, needed someone to take over her class. She had to be out for four months to recuperate from surgery. She recommended me to her principal as her substitute, and the district hired me.

My teaching career was launched.

After Tita Char returned to her class, the Human Resources department gave me teaching assignments from one school to the next.

I was never without a job.

Teaching as a full-time career was something unexpected. It would not have been a surprise had I looked back to my early years in elementary school.

Since I had an engineer for a dad, we had maps all over our house. When I was in the second grade, I would invite all my younger neighbors over. I taught them how to read the names of the cities in the provincial map my dad created.

CHAPTER 8

From Garden to Jungle

I have been teaching fifth grade for several years. Most teachers get a respite in the summer. We need it as it is our time to relax, unwind, rewind, and replenish our energy. It's a time to catch up with all the things we did not get to do throughout the school year—travel, deep clean the house, indulge in our hobbies, or slow down. But for me, I get even busier on my summer breaks. I start every summer by putting a schedule together so I don't waste my precious time.

During one of those summer reprieves, I conjured a plan to write and submit a grant proposal for a school garden with Lowe's "Toolbox for Education." The first day back at school, I shared the idea with my principal and asked for her approval. She gave me a resounding yes! Unknown to me, the district office had already been looking at disassembling unused exercise structures at the northern end of our field because they had become a safety hazard. We identified the venue for the garden.

I went to work and sought the help of a local Master Gardener. He came out, surveyed the area, and helped me put together the budget page. He also gave me referrals and links to other gardens in town. Once completed, I submitted the proposal. The most difficult part was waiting for the results. It could not come soon enough.

To both my principal's and my delight, the proposal got funded, and the garden work began.

That first year our garden was an inspiring delight. Several teachers brought their students to claim a plot. Bean plants, flowers, and cabbages were sprouting—the garden filled with the excited voices of children carrying watering cans and digging with their new trowels. We caught the garden bug!

But years two and three were a flop. These were the years when our school started implementing the Common Core Standards Program. This program is an educational initiative that put together a set of challenging academic expectations for all students. The plan was new to all of us. We had to readjust our way of teaching and learn best practices to implement it. We barely had time for everything it required us to teach. In more ways than one, the saying "when it rains, it pours" proved to be true during this time. The garden needed a great deal of attention. For several months there was so much rain that it prevented classes from tending it. Weeds grew and grew and grew. A jungle was born in the fenced area on the northern end of our suburban school. I had no choice but to ignore the jungle in our school garden.

Unlike real world gardens, our own struggles are difficult to ignore. But we must realize we are not alone. Help is available.

The journey through our struggle with our Fear Giants and the jungle encasing us can seem so daunting and overwhelming. Unlike real world gardens, our own struggles are difficult to ignore. But we must realize we are not alone. Help is available.

After Saul gave David his approval to go after Goliath, Saul dressed David in his tunic, put a coat of armor on him and a bronze helmet on his head. Saul also gave him a sword. But David realized these were not for him.

Tackling the jungle in our school garden—and my jungle of fear—required many different approaches, tools, and strategies. Keep in mind that the "one size fits all" mantra does not always hold true. Not every form of treatment or action point agrees with everyone. We all need to find what fits. I tried several things to get the school garden going. I asked the teachers, students, and parents to help. I had my students work on it once a week. I tried to have contests between classes. Some worked for a period, while others did not last long. What really helped was Sal's and my consistent toil on Saturday mornings.

Employing the Experts

As Sal's weed eater brought instant clearing of the overgrowth around the boxes, we too are given tools to clear up our jungles and slay our giants. David did not get the support from his brothers or the troops, so he went to Saul. I am not a person who has a green thumb or knows a lot about gardens and tools, so I consulted my husband and rallied his help. Physicians dedicate years to studying the art of diagnosing and treating illnesses. They are there for us in our struggles with our health. It is their forte.

I consulted my doctor for help with my anxiety.

Resources

Like the edger in Sal's hands, there are medical tools doctors can use. Do we all need medication? Maybe, maybe not. I took medication when I was younger, and it helped on the occasions when I took it. During my adult years, when I went through menopause, I could not tolerate the same medication I took back then. So, I chose not to use any medication, but I tried to follow other suggestions my doctor gave me, including exercise and improving my diet.

Sal did his job of clearing all the brush that grew around the planter boxes. It was time for more in-depth work—tackling the chaos inside them. Gloves in place, I started pulling the weeds from one of the boxes. The rain from the previous months had softened the soil enough to make pulling easier. Most weeds came off readily, but there were others that I had to fight. Their roots went deep, reaching the bottom part of the enclosures. I searched for weeds that were easiest to pull before I went for the harder ones. Tackling the easy ones gave me a sense of victory. I went from weed to weed, increasing my pile on the side of the box. Then I went back to the more stubborn ones. I struggled to pull a big wad of weeds about a foot in diameter with string-like roots anchored deep, deep into the ground. I looked at my container of tools and found a fork and a trowel. Choosing the trowel, I loosened the soil surrounding the big weed. Finally, the roots let go. I felt a rush of joy as I imagined winning at the game of tug-of-war I used to play when I was a little child.

Weeds grow deep. Their roots go in all directions and establish a strong foothold, competing for water and nutrients with the crops we plant. Our responsibilities and distractions in life can have us sometimes putting our health on the side. They take us away from what is essential; what is a priority, what is life-giving.

I needed to be intentional in pulling the weeds every day, and willing to look outside myself for tools to overcome those with deep roots.

I needed to remain focused on the job at hand. I needed to clean up the jungle inside of me and slay my fears. I needed to be intentional in pulling the weeds every day, and willing to look outside myself for tools to overcome those with deep roots.

Be consistent. According to a study done in 2009 following the habit-formation of 96 people, from the University College London, it takes between 18–254 days to form a habit.[16]

Once we form the habit of implementing the tools and strategies to fight our Fear Giants, we will become the master of our giants instead of it controlling us.

• • •

The fourth year in the garden, I decided to keep the work consistent. I enlisted the help of my class. It was during this time that I unearthed some valuable lessons from our garden that applied to my fight against my Fear Giant. Although it only took him one stone to kill Goliath, David had five stones. For me, each of the five stones David had represents a truth and strategy I learned from my work in the garden. These insights and tools the Lord gave me prepared me when my Fear Giant resurfaced during my menopausal years. I hope they will be as effective weapons for you as they are for me.

Part 3

Acquiring Peace and Healing

"Human beings are partners of the Almighty
in bringing life into the world,
and we are his partners also in healing."

—Ephraim Mirvis

CHAPTER 9

The First Stone—His Perfect Love

Nancy Drew and the Hardy Boys mystery stories were a big part of my book selection in elementary school. An avid reader, as soon as I opened the first page, I couldn't put the book down until the last page. Moving into my teenage years, I pored over every Mills & Boon book I could get my hands on. The stories allowed me to visit places I have never been to and introduced me to characters I had never met. These books influenced my desire to be an aspiring world traveler and add Greece to my destinations' bucket list.

Nowadays, Hallmark movies give me a break from some of the realities of my world. Lounged in comfortable pajamas, sipping hot cocoa in the soothing glow of light from the embers in the fireplace, I watch one or two movies, especially after a long and challenging day at work. These narratives open the floodgates of my tear ducts when the leading lady is at odds with her knight in shining armor. I'm left with butterflies in my stomach when they kiss and pledge their undying love for each other.

Love changes everything.

This recurring theme in Hallmark movies exists not only in fantasy; but also in reality. It is the substance of Dr. Martin Luther King, Jr.'s words, "Darkness cannot drive out darkness; only light can do that. Hate cannot drive out hate; only love can do that."[17]

Love changes everything.

God dubbed David a man after His own heart. Through all of David's imperfections and flaws, God saw David's heart beating for Him with a love that drove him to present himself as Goliath's challenger when he heard the Philistine taunting God's army.

Love changes everything.

John 3:16 says, "For God so loved the world that He gave His one and only Son, that whoever believes in Him shall not perish but have eternal life."

God's love changed everything when He sent His own Son, Jesus Christ, to earth to be the ultimate sacrifice for our sake. Romans 5:8 tells us, "But God demonstrates his own love for us in this: While we were still sinners, Christ died for us." This is the greatest gift. Christ died for us so we can be forgiven and live with Him in eternity.

Love changed our status from guilty to innocent, from condemned to redeemed. He turned our sins from crimson red to wool, from scarlet to white as snow and cleaned our slate (Isaiah 1:18).

God's perfect love casts out fear. The fear of punishment, of being separated from Him, and the fear of death no longer hold a grip on us. The understanding that though our earthly bodies perish, we continue to live and be loved in eternity provides us with hope. It can free us from the greatest fear that we have in our anxiety—the fear of doom and gloom, the fear of death and dying, able to accept and enjoy the abundant life He promised.

We are loved and we have hope.

But there is more good news from 1 John 4:11–21!

When I first read it, I wrestled with understanding these words, "since God so loved us, we also ought to love one another. No one has ever seen God; but if we love one another, God lives in us and *His love is made complete in us* (italics mine)." I prayed and asked the Holy Spirit to help me understand. This is how He unpacked it or me:

> **God's love changed everything when He sent His own Son, Jesus Christ, to earth to be the ultimate sacrifice for our sake.**

God loves us, but because we are sinners,
we could not be in relationship with Him.

PERFECT LOVE

Jesus left the world so He could be with God, the Father. But He didn't leave us helpless, He left us with the Holy Spirit to empower us to live like Him and to love others. The Holy Spirit living in us is our assurance that we are His.

So He sent His Son, Jesus Christ, to die for us so we can be one with Him again and our relationship with Him is restored.

When we surrender our lives to the Lord, He gives His Holy Spirit to live in us and we become His children. John 1:12 states, "Yet to all who did receive Him, to those who believed in His name, He gave the right to become children of God."

We are His. We belong to Him when believe and invite Him into our lives. We can lay claim to our identity. We are His children. We are heirs to His throne. We are the sons and daughters of the most high King.

Because He is in us and is the embodiment of love itself, God gives us the capacity to love others. "No one has ever seen God; but if we love one another, God lives in us and His love is made complete in us" (1 John 4:12). Love enables us to do this through the Holy Spirit in us when we let Him. We cannot see God, but when we love each other, we can see His perfect love manifesting through us. This allows His love to be made complete in us.

Do you see it?

God loves us so much that He includes us in what He wants to accomplish here on Earth. He doesn't need us to achieve what He wants done. He formed the universe and put the stars in place without our help. He can do anything He desires. But He wants to use us to show His perfect love through us by our love for each other!

We are valuable to Him.

He sent His Son Jesus Christ to die on the Cross so we can connect and be in relationship with Him. As we do this, He wants us to connect to each other in love, His perfect love. "His perfect love casts out all fear" (1 John 4:18).

When David first asked the soldiers about Goliath, his brothers mocked him. He did not get their support. So he went to Saul. David was a young man, and Saul doubted that he could fight Goliath. Saul gave David his consent to confront Goliath after David reassured Saul that the Lord would empower him.

As David stood in front of Goliath, he did not fear. He had Saul's approval and he remembered God's faithfulness when he was out in the field tending his father's sheep. He saw God giving him strength as he fought the lion and bear.

I was blessed with parents, family, and relatives who loved and showed their love for me. If you are in the same situation, count your blessings. If that is not the case with you, first remember that God loves you very much. When you accept Him, you become His child. He is your Father, and you have His full support and love. Then seek those who you know truly care about you and love you. Proverbs 12:25 tells us, "Anxiety weighs down the heart, but a kind word cheers it up." So seek those who encourage you. These are the friends and relationships who could help us through the tough times in life and who can rejoice with us in the good.

Knowing we are God's children and the perfect love He has for us, we do not have to fear or live in anxiety.

CHAPTER 10

The Second Stone—Perspective

Kneepads and Cameras

I developed a problem with my knees in my mid-forties. Sal and I were looking at model homes, and on the way up to the second floor, I noticed a pain in my right knee, and I struggled to make it up those steps. The discovery made it obvious to us that a two-story house, even with its advantages, was not for us.

It is not only going up steps that has presented challenges for me. I can only last about five to ten minutes squatting or stooping down to pull weeds before my back, legs, or knees bother me.

During one of my trips to the Dollar Tree store, I found a kneepad and bought one for myself. This turned out to be a valuable tool. The pad allowed me to work in the garden with more ease. I got a better view, and being closer to the weeds made the job faster. One day, while kneeling on my kneepad pulling weeds, a lightbulb went on in my mind. It reminded me of tips I taught my yearbook club members about viewpoint and perspective.

Besides showing my students how to lay out photos and design the yearbook, I modeled for them how to take excellent photos. I coached them on using various points of view for taking pictures: a worm's point of view, taking photographs at eye-level, and a bird's point of view.

According to the dictionary, "Viewpoint is the position from which something or someone is observed."[18] "Perspective, is a particular attitude toward or way of thinking about something."[19] Changing our viewpoint changes our picture, which improves our perspective. This concept can apply to our battle with our Fear Giant and in cleaning up our jungle of symptoms.

However, keep in mind that we may take pictures from the same vantage point, but our interpretation and perspective may turn out different. Our past experiences influence how we see things but it is helpful to consider these vantage points:

Worm's Point of View

On Halloween night, a small, six-year-old boy came to my doorstep for trick-or-treating. Instead of leaving after I gave him candy, he looked at me and said, "You look weird. You have short legs." He entered our house and motioned with his hands, "Your top body is big."

"Oh, okay," was all I could muster.

I didn't know if I should let out a "ha, ha, ha" or a "huh" accompanied with a crease on my brow and a frown. This scenario was a perfect illustration of how viewpoint works. This small boy was looking up at me dressed in a long skirt with a little leg showing, flat flip-flops, and a poofy blouse that added bulkiness to my upper body. Although I am vertically challenged, I know I am well-proportioned. However, he saw me differently because of his vantage point.

Goliath, at nine-feet-nine inches tall, towered above everyone else. Though David was shorter and younger than most of the Israelite soldiers and would have viewed Goliath as even bigger than what the Israelite soldiers saw, his response was different. He remembered the faithfulness and strength God showed him when he faced lions or bears as he protected his family's flock. His vision went beyond Goliath's size. He saw God as greater than Goliath and he responded in confidence and faith.

Kneeling on my kneepad as I pulled weeds made me aware of what my posture should be in relation to God and how I should be as I battle anxiety. From this perspective, our Fear Giant may seem bigger, or the jungle of symptoms may loom over and dwarf us. But

By being on our knees and petitioning God's help, we are accessing a power greater than our fears.

this is also a position of humility before God who is infinitely larger than any giant. 1Peter 5:6 states, "Humble yourselves, therefore, under God's mighty hand, that He may lift you up in due time."

By being on our knees and petitioning God's help, we are accessing a power greater than our fears. Besides, when we are close to the ground, we won't have very far to fall if we faint.

Eye-level

Photographs taken at eye-level mean we are at the same level with the person or thing we are capturing through our lens. I love how Liz Masoner puts it: "Shooting a photo from eye level of the subject is the quickest way to help your viewers connect emotionally with a photo subject."[20] The tendency we have when we realize we have anxiety or irrational fears is to isolate ourselves. Isolation serves to leave more room for us to indulge our negative thoughts and incessant worries.

David's brothers questioned his motives when he inquired about the giant. Instead of becoming discouraged and heading back home, feeling defeated, he went to Saul to support him.

Meeting people and talking to them about my struggles, I discover I am not alone. My perspective changes, my Fear Giant shrinks, because I realize others around me are going through the same thing.

There is strength in numbers.

I approached Diane Bussani, the head of my church's Women's Ministry with a vision I had from the Lord of putting together a retreat for people who struggle with worries and anxieties. Immediately, she got the ball rolling. She invited several ministry leaders to help make the event a reality. After several months of planning and preparation the day of the retreat arrived. There were about a hundred people in attendance. It showed me I was not alone in my struggle. It made me feel others understood.

There is strength in numbers.

Bird's Point of View

Taking pictures of objects or people below us while we are at a higher elevation, is how the bird's point of view works. We need to however keep in mind that even at this position, as human beings, our view is still limited. But not God's. This is His vantage point. He sees everything and knows everything. He is Omniscient, Omnipotent, and Omnipresent. We can't see the full picture when we are going through our fears, but God can. He has a view of everything. He transcends time and space. I remind myself He is in control, knows everything, and has a perfect plan. It changes my perspective from an earthly to a heavenly one. Like David, we need to access memories of His consistent faithfulness in our lives.

As I previously mentioned, my anxiety resurfaced when I was going through menopause. During this time, I was raising my two young children. I became a helicopter mom. In a constant worry-whirl, I not only fretted about myself but about my kids' health, safety, and well-being. Having to work at two different schools, with ten minutes travel time between those two and a hundred students in my caseload, created a very stressful job situation.

By the middle of the day, I no longer appeared like the Energizer Bunny that could keep going, going, and going.

I felt more like a plant dying from thirst but with no drop in sight. Night sweats, hot and cold flashes, vertigo, panic attacks, and sleepless nights heightened the jungle of symptoms I had since I was young. I ran ragged.

I elected to work part-time instead of full-time. However, I did not like that it cut my salary in half. In my bewildered state of mind, I took the Real Estate Certification Exams, passed them, and joined Coldwell Banker as a part-time Realtor. Selling houses was fun and could be profitable, but I found marketing to be a tough gig. There was so much competition which added to my stress. I had jumped from the frying pan into the fire.

The Fear Giant and jungle in me was at its pinnacle. I feared driving or going shopping alone because of fears that I might develop a sudden onset of vertigo—fear after fear stacked on top of each other. Most of the time, my husband had to act as my designated driver.

I became very introspective and hypersensitive to every symptom I felt. I translated pain in my jaw, aches in my back, or a migraine headache as either a heart attack or a brain tumor or any other thing a hypochondriac could conjure.

The emergency room nurses and doctors were no longer acquaintances but friends because of my frequent visits. The ER offered me comfort as well as dread. Comfort because I knew if something major happened to me, I was already with the doctors, nurses, and other professionals who could take care of me. Dread stemmed from the thought of being told I was experiencing a heart attack or something serious and life-threatening. These thoughts intensified the shakiness of my hands, rapid heart rate, and blood pressure.

After every ER visit, I followed up with my regular physician. He listened without judging me. He told me he believed in me and my capabilities and his belief had a positive impact on the perception I had of myself. I knew I had a voice in my treatment plan. With this confidence, I had clarity of what I required. I requested a referral to a behavior analyst. I saw the therapist, and three appointments were all I needed.

During one of those visits, I expressed my concerns to her.

"I feel like it is taking me so long to get over the things I am going through."

The answer she gave me made an incredible impact in my thinking and in my recovery.

"Cecille, ask yourself, what can you do today you could not do last week, last month, last year?"

This opened my eyes. Redirecting my consciousness toward what I had already accomplished instead of dwelling on the enormity of my symptoms led me in the right path.

Retrain our brain.

Based on what we learned about the pathophysiology of anxiety, it would do us good to retrain our brain. Looking at our fight using different perspectives and seeing it from varying angles is a good start.

My students and I were working in the garden one morning when I heard a loud, "Eeeewe!" and saw one of the girls shaking her hands and running around the planter boxes. I discovered she unearthed some worms. Knowing this was a teachable moment, I explained to all of my students the value of earthworms.

Our anxieties can sometimes become our own "Eeeewe!" moments. Instead of hiding them and running away from them, we can accept that fears, worries, the storms, and challenges we encounter are a part of life. Our fears can also guard us from getting into dangerous situations. Dolly Parton once said, "Storms make trees take deeper roots."[21]

Amid our storms or moments when our giants seem to take us in a death hold, we need to see things through all the different perspectives available to us. We need to see the glass half-full instead of half-empty.

It is essential to understand that every successful experience we have achieved fighting against our Fear Giants goes into our memory. As we repeat these experiences, new pathways in our Limbic System form and our confidence in our ability to win grows. That's why we need to celebrate our victories. Romans 5:3–5 tells us, "Not only so, but we also glory in our sufferings, because we know that suffering produces perseverance; perseverance character, and character, hope. And hope does not put us to shame, because God's love has been poured out into our hearts through the Holy Spirit, who has been given to us."

"Storms make trees take deeper roots."
—Dolly Parton

With each visit to the emergency room, my brain was being retrained. I learned that not all the increased heart rate, sweaty palms, and lightheadedness I had were symptoms of heart attacks or something serious. This awareness allowed me to evaluate the source of my symptoms logically. And if I still doubted or continued to be concerned, I knew there was always help available for me.

The Women of Faith posted in one of their Instagrams, "When the roots are deep, there is no reason to fear the wind." When the winds of change, fear, and challenge blow our way, we muster all our strength and bend our knees in prayer and anticipation. We look to the heavens knowing He who sits in the Heavenly throne is in control and bigger than our giant. Then we seek help and support from those around us and focus on what is true, excellent, noble, lovely, admirable, praiseworthy, pure, and right (Philippians 4:8). We will transform our thinking as we wait and are still, knowing and acknowledging that the One by our side is God.

Progress may have been gradual, but any movement is better than no movement at all.

Movement happens when we look at things differently. It allows us to adjust the way we approach the jungle of symptoms we have when our Fear Giants attack our mind. We no longer are stagnant and stay at status quo, we move toward transformation. Perspective is essential for this to occur.

Perspective changes our process and moves us to progress.

CHAPTER 11

The Third Stone—Praise

My excited students eagerly sat in a circle with crisscrossed legs on the green carpeted floor of our classroom, waiting to see what we would do. Every year it amazes me that I am able to contain their excitement, to give me thirty minutes for my end-of-the-school-year tradition, before the last-day festivities begin. We go around the circle complimenting or thanking each other out loud. They praise their classmates for who they are or thank them for how they have positively impacted them. After defining what a compliment is, I explain other guidelines, making sure they understand that everyone needs to receive a praise or appreciation from someone. Usually comments like, "I like your dress," "Thank you for being a good friend," or "You are smart," start the ball rolling.

I have taken this up a notch the past two years. Instead of just saying it out loud, my students also write their compliments or gratitude. They write it down on stationery I have prepared for each one of them with their names on top using stickers. This way, they have affirmations they can read and reread. I love doing this because it reminds my students of the good others see in them. We all love to hear something positive about us or what we do, right?

Often, I mix up praise and thanksgiving. The Merriam-Webster dictionary defines the verb "praise," as "to express a favorable judgment of: COMMEND" and "to glorify (a god or saint) especially by the attribution of perfections".[22] As a noun, it is defined as "an expression of approval: COMMENDATION" or "worship—to honor or show reverence for a divine being or supernatural power."[23] The same dictionary defines "thanksgiving" as "an act of giving thanks" or "a prayer which expresses gratitude."[24]

Why Praise?

Developing an attitude of praise throughout the day is one way of changing our perspective. Psalm 35:28 says, "My tongue will proclaim your righteousness, your praises all day long." Instead of focusing on our Fear Giants, we dwell on God's awesomeness and His ability to take care of our worries. We allow Him to show us what He could do, stepping back and letting Him take control. In the story of King Jehoshaphat, it was after King Jehoshaphat and the people of Judah and Jerusalem started singing and praising God that the Lord acted to defeat their enemies. Second Chronicles documents this event. "Early in the morning, they left for the Desert of Tekoa. As they set out, Jehoshaphat stood and said, 'Listen to me, Judah and people of Jerusalem! Have faith in the Lord your God and you will be upheld; have faith in his prophets and you will be successful.' After consulting the people, Jehoshaphat appointed men to sing to the Lord and to praise him for the splendor of his holiness as they went out at the head of the army, saying: "Give thanks to the Lord, for His love endures forever." As they began to sing and praise, the Lord set ambushes against the men of Ammon and Moab and Mount Seir who were invading Judah, and they were defeated" (2 Chronicles 20:18-22). II Kings 19:15 talks about how Hezekiah prayed to the Lord: "Lord, the God of Israel, enthroned between the cherubim, you alone are God over all the kingdoms of the earth. You have made heaven and earth."

Like Hezekiah, we praise God to acknowledge that He is God. We honor and revere Him. We glean this even from the prayer Jesus taught His disciples. In the Lord's prayer, it starts with, "Our Father in heaven, hallowed be your name." We praise Him for His attributes. Hallowed means to revere.[25]

The book of Psalms offers more reasons why we praise the Lord. Psalm 22:3 says, "Because your love is better than life, my lips will glorify you. I will praise you as long as I live, and in your name, I will lift up my hands." Psalm 100:3 also tells us, "Know that the Lord is God. It is he who made us, and we are his; we are his people, the sheep of his pasture." We are His. To praise God, we need to know Him and His character. Jeremiah 29:13 tells us, "You will seek me and find me when you seek me with all your heart." It begins with our hearts seeking Him.

Gratitude

Weeds abounded in the garden on one of my visits. I started pulling again. As I removed ugly weeds, flowers growing from bulbs planted the past year surfaced. Underneath the overgrowth were treasures of beauty that brought back the words my behavioral therapist said to me about my journey to recovery: "Look at what you are able to do now that you weren't able to do then." Celebrating both significant and minor successes is imperative. Celebrating the achievements we have experienced fighting our Fear Giants is essential. With celebration comes thanksgiving.

Gratitude is good medicine.

Celebrating both significant and minor successes is imperative.

One summer, we toured our niece and her friend around Old Sacramento. While strolling through the cobbled streets and charming shops, I noticed what I thought was a statue of a man sitting on one of the benches. He wore a Hawaiian shirt, his eyes closed, his face taut, smooth and shiny. I was trying to get our niece and her friend to sit down next to him so I could take their picture, when suddenly, he moved. That startled and scared me. I scurried past him, afraid he would ask me for something (talk about assumptions).

I was about three stores past him when the Holy Spirit spoke to my heart about offering him food or a drink. I retraced my steps back to the ice cream shop right in front of where he sat and asked the owner of the store if they had drinks. He pointed to the soda fountain. With a bit of trepidation, I approached the man sitting on the bench and asked if he wanted a drink. He smiled at me and said he would love a strawberry ice cream. I signaled for him to enter the shop and paid for his ice cream. With a sparkle in his eye and a broad smile, he reached one hand to touch my shoulder and said, "Thank you and bless you."

Like an eagle, my heart soared. I smiled back at him, and any traces of fear or discomfort I first had disappeared into thin air.

Gratitude changes our attitude.

Many stories of thankfulness and gratitude are in the Bible. Throughout His life on earth, Jesus showed and stressed the importance of showing appreciation and thanksgiving. In Matthew 15:36–37, after receiving the seven loaves and the fish from His disciples, Jesus gave thanks before He broke it down and gave it back to them to distribute to the multitude. Luke 17:14–18 talks about ten lepers whom Jesus healed after following what He told them to do. Out of the ten, only one came back to thank and glorify God. Jesus asked the Samaritan man who went back, "Were not all ten cleansed? Where are the other nine? Has no one returned to give praise to God except this foreigner?" (Luke 17:17–18).

• • •

The Value of Music

I mix up praise and thanksgiving when I pray because praising God and honoring Him for who He is naturally leads me to seeing the goodness and blessings He has given me. The good that He does is a by-product of His character. He is a good God. Psalm 107:1 says, "Give thanks to the Lord, for he is good; his love endures forever." Psalm 34:8 further affirms this truth,

"Taste and see that the Lord is good; blessed is the one who takes refuge in him."

Throughout my fight with my Fear Giant, I have learned to take refuge in the Lord. He has shown His goodness and faithfulness in seeing me through them. James 1:17 tells us, "Every good and perfect gift is from above, coming down from the Father of the heavenly lights, who does not change like shifting shadows." My peace, strength, healing, and perseverance all come from Him. As I praise Him, I recognize and acknowledge the work of His hands. Like a river flowing in one direction, that recognition naturally proceeds to thanksgiving. Besides praise and thanksgiving, singing to the Lord expresses worship. King Jehoshaphat and his men sang and praised God before they faced their enemies.

A friend posted on her Facebook page how her family was moving to another state, and expressed her disappointment that they had not even explored their current city. Have you seen pictures posted of beautiful sceneries that you did not know existed in your area, right there in your own backyard? Often, this happens because we don't really think about what we have. Sometimes we take things for granted. One thing I took for granted was the value of music. My perception and value for music changed after an experiment I conducted out of necessity and triggered by an article I read.

I used to have about twenty-five orchids of different varieties inside our house. I found watering was easier and less messy outside rather than transporting each one of them to and from the kitchen sink. One day, I moved all of them to the backyard outside our

bedroom door, and under the umbrella of the beauti-
fully cascading pink wisteria blooms on our pergola.
Unfortunately, that was also the day when the tem-
peratures in Sacramento hit a record-breaking high of
110 degrees. When I got home from work, the devas-
tating scene of my scorched orchids greeted me. After
saying a prayer to the Lord to preserve my orchids,
I painstakingly transferred all of them to our bath-
tub. I showered them with water, talked to them, and
soothed them with classical music playing throughout
the entire night and the next day. An article I found
online inspired the actions I took. The post detailed
how Giancarlo Cignozzi, an Italian wine grower in
the hills of Montalcino, Tuscany, used classical music
to encourage the growth and abundance of his grapes.
He found that those grapevines that were closest
to the source of classical music produced healthier,
sweeter grapes compared to the vines farthest from the
music. He also found that there was a decrease in bug
infestation. His theory was that the music confused
the bugs, and they could not breed.[26]

My orchids survived and came back to health. I
don't know if it was my prayer, the water, the music,
or the combination of all three that brought about
this result.

Although it was not an overnight cure, I was
overjoyed.

Now throughout the day at our house, there is
music. Not just any kind, but music that Sal and I
enjoy, and which uplifts us. Music that remind us of
God's faithfulness and His character, giving us an
attitude of worship. If we are not home, then the dogs
get to listen to it.

Although I like solitude and silence, most times, I enjoy having praise music playing. It helps keep my heart singing the whole day. It also keeps my focus on what is true, right, noble, praiseworthy, pure, and excellent. It refrains my brain from focusing on the negative or fixating on what causes me fear, anxiety, and worry.

Research shows the connection between listening to music and our moods and mental well-being. The following is a partial list of what the American Music Therapy Association finds to be the benefits of using music therapy:

- "Make positive changes in mood and emotional states

- Have a sense of control over life through successful experiences

- Enhance awareness of self and environment

- Develop coping and relaxation skills

- Support healthy feelings and thoughts

- Develop independence and decision-making skills" [27]

According to the Center for American Military Music Opportunities or CAMMO, a site that provides performance opportunities for veterans and active duty service members, "Research has demonstrated that music and rhythm affects multiple areas of the brain simultaneously, and the brain that engages in music is actually changed by that engagement. Music can help build new neural connections in the brain through experience and exposure, thus improving rehabilitative potential and the ability of the brain to 'rewire' itself after trauma or injury, allowing individuals to lead more productive and functional lives."[28]

Not only do we please and move God when we praise, thank, and sing to Him, doing these things helps us in our fight. Praise, gratitude, and music changes not only our perspective but also retrains our brain. It keeps our sling by our side as Colossians 3:16 points out, "Let the message of Christ dwell among you richly as you teach and admonish one another with all wisdom, through psalms, hymns and songs from the Spirit, singing to God with gratitude in your hearts."

We praise, thank, and sing our way to victory in our fight!

CHAPTER 12

The Fourth Stone— Passion & Prayer

Ferdinand Foch, the commander of the Allied forces in World War I and considered by many to be responsible for its victory[29] said, "The most powerful weapon on earth is the human soul on fire." This is passion. The Merriam-Webster Dictionary defines "passion" as "a strong liking or desire for or devotion to some activity, object, or concept."[30]

Fear, anxiety, and worry are strong negative emotions. We need to counter these with equally strong positive emotions. This is where your passion comes in.

However, it should not only be a passion that could benefit you but those around you as well.

What are you passionate about?

After my daughter's wedding reception, I found leftover flower arrangements in three bird cages. I arranged them in two different vases and took them to a local convalescent hospital close to the high school my children used to attend. I talked to the intake specialist there and told her what I wanted to do with the flowers. She beamed and took me to the rooms of two patients. One of them had not had family or guests for a long time. Her contagious smile displayed her appreciation. Farther down the hall, she ushered me into a dark, gloomy room. The drapes were closed. The specialist pulled the curtains back to bring in the light from the morning sun. I laid the vase with the arrangement of pink and red roses, brimmed by eucalyptus leaves, on top of a table as the specialist told the resident they were for her. Although the patient's response was a whispered "Thank you," the exuberance in my heart was loud enough.

I cried on my way home. Feelings of joy lifted my heart as I heard a voice inside me say, "Flowers for Elders." It marked the day I founded my nonprofit— an organization that provides flower arrangements repurposed from weddings or memorial services and given to patients in convalescent facilities. The euphoria I experienced was the same one I found when, as an elementary school student, I used my meager twenty-cent allowance to purchase a rose from our neighborhood grower and then gave it to any of my classmates celebrating her birthday. The passion for brightening someone's day with flowers had always been there.

When we look past our own problems and concerns and look at others' needs and well-being, we get even more than we are giving. These rewards are treasures, like the flowers covered in weeds in our garden. Luke 6:38 notes, "Give, and it will be given to you. A good measure, pressed down, shaken together and running over, will be poured into your lap. For with the measure you use, it will be measured to you."

Standing Strong Together in Spirit

We can achieve robust giving in the confines of our closet, our own home, or in our heart at any time of the day. We call this giving an intercessory prayer. Ephesians 6:18 states, "And pray in the Spirit on all occasions with all kinds of prayers and requests. With this in mind, be alert and always keep on praying for all the Lord's people."

We need to stand in the gap for each other.

We are urged to pray in the Spirit at all times about everything and for all the Lord's people. As I have people praying for me and with me, I am also praying for them and others. Not only does this keep us from thinking only of our own struggles, it connects us in another dimension to those whom we know and love, and even those who are strangers.

We need to stand in the gap for each other.

When we pray for others, we are connecting the person we are praying about with our most powerful Lord. We are petitioning Him on their behalf. This act of putting our own needs aside to lift the needs of others is love perfected in us, our agape love.

I was in the middle of teaching a class when I suddenly noticed light flashes appearing at the side of my face. Concerned, I dialed the advice nurse. She relayed the message to my doctor. Worried I was developing retinal detachment, he scheduled me with no hesitation for an emergency appointment with an ophthalmologist.

Thinking this medical emergency could be a possibility worried me. I prayed, then took my phone out, texted, e-mailed, and messaged my family and friends. My message read: "I have an emergency appointment with an ophthalmologist tomorrow just to make sure I am not experiencing what could be a retinal detachment. Will you please pray for me? Thanks."

Not only did it help that people responded letting me know they were praying, it helped me to know I was not going through this alone. Sal could not take the day off to take me to my appointment, so my neighbor volunteered. I knew I had all my family and friends who were praying for me with me in spirit as I went to my appointment.

Several scriptures talk about this. Ephesians 6:18 says, "Praying at all times in the Spirit, with all prayer and supplication. To that end keep alert with all perseverance, making supplication for all the saints." I also love what Ecclesiastes 4:9–12 tells us: "Two are better than one, because they have a good reward for their toil. For if they fall, one will lift up his fellow. But woe to him who is alone when he falls and has not another to lift him up! Again, if two lie together, they keep warm, but how can one keep warm alone? And though a man might prevail against one who is alone, two will withstand him—a threefold cord is not quickly broken." Matthew 18:20 solidifies this truth, "For where two or three gather in my name, there am I with them."

I have always wanted to wear contact lenses instead of being burdened by glasses. The extreme sensitivity I have with anything that comes close to my eyes has prevented me from being able to wear contacts. So, I expected I would not do well during the exam. To my surprise, the bright, blinding light piercing my pupils and the doctor stretching every corner and angle of my eyes during the exam did not bother me, I felt serenity and peace no giant could penetrate.

Recently, one of my best friends texted me and asked me to pray for her and the situation she was facing. I texted her back reassuring her I was praying that moment. I wanted to give her a scripture verse to hold on to and came across Deuteronomy 3:22. "Do not be afraid of them; the Lord your *God Himself will fight for you* (italics mine)."

As I was getting ready to send this to her, I received this text from her,

"Check this out. Verse of the day: 'The Lord shall fight for you and ye shall hold your peace. Exodus 14:14 KJV'"

I could not believe my eyes. At the same moment, when we were seeking the Lord's Word, He gave us the same word from different places and translations.

We have an unbelievably amazing God who cares about every detail of our lives and knows exactly what we need!

Praying in accord prevents pesky Fear Giants from robbing our chance for peace.

CHAPTER 13

The Fifth Stone—Perseverance

When I accepted Jesus as my Savior, I immediately felt His peace, but the symptoms of my fears and anxiety did not miraculously disappear. I still experienced them, but the confidence I had in Him and the peace He gave me during those moments allowed me to continue to enjoy life.

God could radically and instantly heal us. He could also elect to have us continue our daily battle but provide us with day-to-day strength and wisdom to persevere and proclaim victory over our fears and anxieties. Like some of the events in the life of the Israelites, sometimes we can struggle for years. Their battles and wanderings or the sufferings of people in the Bible witness to us about this. Take the story of the woman who suffered from a bleeding disorder for twelve years (Matthew 9:20–22) or the story of the man who was disabled for thirty-eight years and was healed by Jesus at the pool of Bethesda (John 5:1–8). Their trials were not short-lived.

Our trust and confidence in God's ability to heal or strengthen us as we deal with our Fear Giants is a process. If we are to hold on to Him for help navigating through the difficulties in life, we need to know Him and be well-grounded in His Word. By doing this, when the storms in life come, when the worrying starts and the fears threaten our peace, they will not blow us away. We have to have both head and heart knowledge of Him and His ways. How do we achieve this? Here are some ways to help us.

Rooted in Him

On one of our trips to Hawaii, I bought a plumeria cutting to bring home to the mainland. The directions had me soak the cut end in a small container of water. It instructed me to change the water daily until roots developed. My cue to plant it in a pot of porous soil was when I saw that the roots were plentiful.

The science lesson I taught my students further supports this process. A plant starts with the seed or a cutting. When planted, it has to develop roots. Otherwise it won't survive. The root sucks up water and nutrients for the entire plant. The more abundant and deep roots develop, the better chance for the plant to be deeply-seated and grow. If its roots are sparse and shallow, the plant could easily fall and die.

In the "Parable of the Sower," Jesus talks about the state of a person's heart and the outcome when he heard the Gospel (Matthew 13:1–23). He used the illustration of a farmer sowing seeds and how those seeds fared as they fell on different types of soil. This parable addresses the state of our hearts, our faith, and relationship with Him and His Word. An illustration Jesus made of the material the seeds ended up in was rocky ground (Matthew 13:5–6, 20–21). Because the rocky terrain did not have much soil, the plants grew but did not develop deep roots, and eventually did not survive.

The soil is the condition of our heart. God looks at and knows our heart. God knows what is best for us. (Isaiah 55:8–9). Are we willing to listen to Him, and be open to His leading, wisdom, and guidance? Or do we just go with what other people suggest or use our own ideas and ways without consulting Him? Do we have a quiet and contrite heart that pleases the Lord? (1 Peter 3:4). Are we studying His Word, so we know Him more and grow in our faith in Him?

Succulents are easy to grow. They require low maintenance. However, there are some guidelines to help them thrive well. Although they only need to be watered once a week, when these plants are soaked in water, they get maximum hydration. They also need to be drained well. That is why planting them using a well-draining soil in a pot with a drainage hole is preferable.[31]

Roots are essential for plants to thrive and grow. This statement applies to us and our confidence in the Lord, too. Being rooted in the Lord means we are soaked in His Word and are applying the lessons we learn from the Word to our daily lives. We become doers of His Word and not just hearers (James 1:22). This is building a strong and solid foundation in Him.

Connected to Him

God loves us, and in His love, we can rest in the assurance that no matter what happens, He is with us, and His peace is available to us. We develop confidence in His promises by remaining and growing in Him. John 15:5 says, "I am the vine; you are the branches. If you remain in me and I in you, you will bear much fruit; apart from me you can do nothing."

Jesus was in the presence of a Samaritan woman fetching water from a well. He asked her for a drink. The woman gave Him water which started their conversation, eventually leading Jesus to tell her He was the source of Living Water. Jesus sustains us, and His provision keeps flowing and never runs dry. The Lord is the source of a non-ending supply for our needs and of peace, and His Holy Spirit is the source of our strength and power. Like a weed eater needing gas or a power outlet to do its work, we need to be constantly linked to the One who has a steady supply of everything we require to fight our Fear Giants. Our slings need the power behind its strength and force.

We must remain connected to Him to continue receiving the nourishment to advance our growth. Studying His Word, praying, and engaging in fellowship with other believers can assure us of this. Also, we can continuously surrender ourselves to Him daily and remember His promises and faithfulness to us in the past.

> **We must remain connected to Him to continue receiving the nourishment to advance our growth.**

Waiting on Him

It takes time and consistency to remain steadfast in God's Word and to truly trust Him. Like a runner, we have to exercise our muscles of faith every day and keep building our stamina, lest we grow weak and weary.

We need to implement the techniques of claiming and sharing God's perfect love, changing our perspective and focus, praising, praying, and indulging our passions to benefit not just us but others also. Then sufficient time is necessary to develop a habit of using the tools we have learned to fight against anxieties and fears.

Sal and I recently decided to be more intentional about living a healthier lifestyle. We embarked on a journey of eliminating some carbohydrates and sugar from our diet and to start exercising. We took a baseline measurement of our weight. Two days after starting this regimen, we stepped back onto the scales. Not a good idea! The numbers did not tip over to our desired outcome. It was too soon to check.

It is important to implement and practice the strategies we have to help us fight our Fear Giants for an appropriate period of time for us to be able to test their effectiveness. We also need to remind ourselves that we can set our plans and goals, but God's perfect timing supersedes ours. Proverbs 16:9 tells us, "In their hearts, humans plan their course, but the Lord establishes their steps." Ecclesiastes 3:1 reminds us that there is a time for everything.

Waiting on Him and trusting Him will not be in vain. Lamentations 3:25–26, "The Lord is good to those whose hope is in him, to the one who seeks him; it is good to wait quietly for the salvation of the Lord," and Proverbs 3:5–6, "Trust in the Lord with all your heart and lean not on your own understanding; in all your ways submit to him, and he will make your paths straight," assures us of this. He is faithful!

Remembering God's Faithfulness

The famous poet Ralph Waldo Emerson said, "What lies behind you and what lies in front of you, pales in comparison to what lies inside of you."[32] When the going gets tough, we keep going by remembering who we belong to and what He has given us. Our source of strength is the Lord, our power through His Holy Spirit. We keep His faithfulness in the forefront of our minds, which will increase our confidence that He is able and will see us through.

When going through trying times, it is easy to forget what God has brought us through. Scripture shows God reminding people of the importance of remembering His faithfulness. The story of the Israelites as they traveled from Shitthim (Joshua 3–4:1–7) is an example.

They were fleeing from the men of the king of Jericho. The Jordan River was between where they were and the land the Lord had promised them. The Lord instructed Joshua, their leader, to tell the Levitical priests carrying the ark of the covenant to step into and stand in the river. As promptly as they followed his directions, a miracle transpired. "Now the Jordan is at flood stage all during harvest. As soon as the priests who carried the ark reached the Jordan and their feet touched the water's edge, the water from upstream stopped flowing. It piled up in a heap a great distance away, at a town called Adam near Zarethan, while the water flowing down to the Sea of the Arabah (that is, the Dead Sea) was cut off. So, the people crossed over opposite Jericho" (Joshua 3:15–16).

The Lord told Joshua to choose twelve men, each one representing each of the twelve tribes of Judah. They were to go back to the middle of the river where the priests stood with the ark and pick up stones and bring them back to Jericho. These stones were to serve as a memorial of the miracle God performed, an Ebenezer.

They were instructed to go to the middle of the river.

Seriously, why the middle of the river? Couldn't they just have picked up the stones from the edge? I could imagine these twelve men going back halfway between the men they were fleeing, and freedom. Did they feel afraid once again?

Going to the middle of the river is equivalent to asking me to rehash one of my anxiety scenarios. Reliving our anxieties is painful and uncomfortable. In the back of our minds, is the haunting voice that questions, *"Will this hurl me once more into a full-blown anxiety attack?"*

I believe God wants us to go back to the place where His miracle occurred to keep us believing and remind us that His sustenance is sure.

Joshua 4:3, 6–7 continues, "and command them, saying, 'Take twelve stones from here out of the midst of the Jordan, from the very place where the priests' feet stood firmly, and bring them over with you and lay them down in the place where you lodge tonight— that this may be a sign among you. When your children ask in time to come, 'What do those stones mean to you?' then you shall tell them that the waters of the Jordan were cut off before the ark of the covenant of the Lord. When it passed over the Jordan, the waters of the Jordan were cut off. So these stones shall be to the people of Israel a memorial forever.'"

I believe God wants us to go back to the place where His miracle occurred to keep us believing and remind us that His sustenance is sure.

We need to lay down stones of remembrance of God's faithfulness wherever we are in our journey. These Ebenezers will serve as a reminder of the miracles He has done in our lives and as an encouragement for us to persevere.

Every building is built up stone upon stone, brick upon brick. As we lay down the stones, we build our confidence in Him to see us through.

These stepping-stones of remembrance will keep us going when it seems like there is no end to what we are going through. Hebrews 12:1–2 says, "Therefore, since we are surrounded by such a great cloud of witnesses, let us throw off everything that hinders and the sin that so easily entangles. And let us run with perseverance the race marked out for us, fixing our eyes on Jesus, the pioneer and perfecter of faith. For the joy set before him he endured the cross, scorning its shame, and sat down at the right hand of the throne of God."

He will perfect our faith. The knowledge of God's faithfulness will keep us from growing weary and losing heart when we are time and time again visited by our fears and anxieties.

Fixing our eyes on Jesus and the faithfulness He has shown us will keep us running toward our goal of slaying our Fear Giants.

Daily, I gather my "Stones of Remembrance" by jotting down what God has done for me for the day. My journal includes: My prayers, His answers to my prayers, and how He has helped me overcome and manage my anxiety and other nuggets of discernment He gave me. I go back to these when situations that bring me fear or make me anxious confront me or when I go through other challenges. Knowing God was faithful during those times gave me confidence He would always be faithful. Malachi 3:6 states "I the Lord do not change. So you, the descendants of Jacob, are not destroyed."

God is the same yesterday, today, and forever.

• • •

Enhancing the Soil

Tending gardens involve tilling the soil and using strategies to fertilize plants and minimize weeds and pest damage. What has this got to do with our fight against our Fear Giants and our jungle?

Like fertilizers that add to and improve the soil of a garden, some strategies, techniques, and things we do, help us sustain our oasis of peace. Eliminating things which do not help, are our pest and weed controls that thwart invaders competing with crops for essentials to healthy growth. When we are rooted in and connected with Christ, waiting on Him and remembering His faithfulness, He continues to give us wisdom to discern ways to help us persevere. These strategies, techniques, and healthy choices are our fertilizers. Let's look at some that have helped me and might help you.

Cultivating Friendships

An article by the Mayo Clinic Staff stated that "Good friends are good for your health." I find this to be true in my life. I would be amiss if I did not acknowledge that having a strong network of friends has helped me in my fight against my Fear Giants. Looking back throughout my elementary, high school, college, and post-graduate years, friends constantly enveloped me. The time invested together and the experiences we shared, established our deep ties. Though distance has set us apart and the seasons of our lives have changed, the strong bond we developed remained unaltered. Despite forming new friendships with others, I nurtured not only my new relationships but also those formed during my growing-up years. The distance would have made it hard but social media has resolved that. All of us try to keep in touch to encourage and support each other via messages, emails, or Facebook posts. My high school friends who live in the United States, some of whom have been my classmates since my preschool years, spend time together at least once a year.

True friendships are difficult to develop and maintain. You need to be intentional and invest your time in them. It is also when times are tough and challenging that you can find those who truly care and love you. When you do—keep them, nurture them, and love them. They are treasures that you never want to let go.

Benefits of Fresh Air

One question my students had to wrestle with as we studied ecosystems and the food web was, "What do plants eat?"

"Dirt!" one student yelled out.

"Water," another student quipped.

As we performed an experiment, discussed, and watched the accompanying video to the program we were using, we learned that the biggest source of food for plants is air. We have a symbiotic relationship with plants. Plants give us oxygen, and we give them carbon dioxide. Therefore, we need to be mindful of conserving our natural resources.

Most of plants' weight and mass come from air. Stomatas are minute openings in the plants' leaves that take in air. When these are covered, and plants cannot access air, they die.[33] Air is essential for plants to survive. Similarly, we cannot survive without oxygen, and a breath of fresh air can do our human body good. Common strategies medical professionals recommend to ease stress are deep breathing techniques and breath focus. When we are stressed, our breathing becomes fast and shallow. Deep breathing allows us to get more air into our bodies and is done by slowly breathing in and out through our nose. To check that we are doing this correctly, we place one hand in our belly and one hand on our chest. Breathing in, we feel our belly rise more than our chest. Breathing out causes our belly to lower. While performing deep breathing exercises, we can also picture a word or phrase that helps us relax. As we breathe in, we visualize and tell ourselves that we are breathing in peace and calm. As we breathe out, we imagine and tell ourselves we are breathing out stress and tension.[34] Another visualization technique I learned is picturing a peaceful scene. For me, this would be a calm ocean or a foggy morning. How about you? What pictures calm you?

Sal and I go for drives every Saturday or Sunday when we are free. After a week of working hard, we play hard. Playing hard for us means going for a drive, sightseeing, and exploring places we have never been to or going back to our favorite getaways. We delight in being out in the open, experiencing and enjoying nature. Not only does this enable us to be amidst what provides our oxygen, it also gives us a chance to indulge in our shared hobby of photography. Because we do this often, we keep our expenses at a budget by putting together a picnic basket or go through healthy but cheap drive-through restaurants.

Water

I used to visit a massage therapist for a back injury I sustained in school. At each session, he stressed the importance of my water intake. I believed him, but the problem I had with drinking the prescribed amount of water throughout the school day was that as a teacher I did not have the liberty to just leave my class anytime to use the restroom. I couldn't drink more than my bladder could hold for a specified period.

The human body is made up of 50-78% water depending on age, gender, and fitness level. The moment we feel thirsty, we have already lost about 2 to 3% of our body's water. At 1% dehydration, our mental performance and physical coordination go down.[35] No wonder I used to get headaches after school when I have not had enough water to drink during the day and how it went away when I drank water on my way home. Making sure our water intake is adequate keeps our minds and bodies performing at their optimum levels.

Adding what our body needs

The sun felt hot as I walked across the blacktop. Feeling despondent because of my lack of energy, I had my head down.

"Hi, Cecille. Are you OK?" Evie Baker, a colleague asked on her way to the office.

Looking up, I replied, "Not really."

"What's wrong?"

Misty-eyed, I blurted out my struggle.

She encouraged me by telling me that she had the same jungle of symptoms while going through menopause. Then she shared with me how she had to pay attention to what she ate. The most important information she shared had to do with bananas. She discovered that having a daily banana calmed her down. That started my banana regimen.

Bananas are natural beta-blockers. When we are in a threatening situation, adrenaline or epinephrine gets pumped into our blood from the adrenal glands to help us survive. This event triggers all the physiological symptoms we feel, our jungle. The adrenaline binds to beta-receptors in our sympathetic nervous system and triggers an increase in heart rate, blood pressure, and the pumping of oxygenated blood to our muscles to prepare our legs to run were there a need to flee.

Since the composition in bananas block beta receptors, adrenaline cannot bind to them, which prevent our pulse rate and blood pressure from spiking up. Bananas are also potassium-packed. Potassium is a mineral in our body which helps to keep our heartbeat regular, our brains oxygenated, and regulates our body's water balance. When we feel stressed, the potassium level in our body decreases. Eating bananas helps replenish the potassium we lost.

Besides potassium, bananas are rich in magnesium and the protein tryptophan. Both increase our serotonin level. Serotonin is a natural mood stabilizer. It keeps us from being depressed. We also find vitamin B in bananas. This vitamin helps calm the nervous system.[36]

Having a banana not only prevented my jungle from growing, but it also curtailed the Fear Giant from flustering me. It calmed my nerves.

Eating a banana a day helped me and is something you could try, but be sure to check with your physician and get his advise and approval, especially if you are taking medications.

Plants need six primary nutrients: carbon, hydrogen, oxygen, nitrogen, phosphorus, and potassium. Human beings need nutrients, minerals, and vitamins, too. We need to make sure we are eating healthy and well-balanced meals to keep our systems going.

Exercising

Exercise fosters the release of powerful chemicals in our brain called endorphins. Endorphins lift our spirits and well-being. Besides the changes that occur in our brain, physical activity releases the tension build-up in our body and helps our muscles to relax. It breaks the cycle that occurs when we are thinking fearful thoughts and experiencing their related symptoms.

Putting together and complying with a consistent exercise routine eluded me. The constant "fight-flight" mode was not only harmful to my heart, but it also zapped the strength out of me. I wanted to exercise but lacked stamina. Can you relate?

Instead of beating myself up because of this failure, I engaged in things I could do successfully. Like that of a toddler learning to walk, I took baby steps. I started with ten-minute walks with Sal. As my energy increased, so did the length of my walk. Stretches became a part of my routine done in the comfort of our home. To keep us persistent, we need to take baby steps and give ourselves grace when we stumble.

> **Like that of a toddler learning to walk, I took baby steps.**

Adequate Sleep

I tossed and turned. But sleep would not come. I needed to rest. My full schedule the next day included an early morning staff meeting, teaching my 5th graders from nine-to-three, cooking dinner, and putting together fifteen floral arrangements that I had to drop off at church that evening. I glimpsed at the clock by my husband's side of the bed. 12:40.

Lord, please give me sleep. I have an early morning meeting and have fifteen floral arrangements to put together after work tomorrow, plus help with decorating at church. I prayed as if the Lord didn't know.

But. Sleep. Still. Eluded. Me.

I recited part of Psalm 127:2 and claimed it for myself, "for He grants sleep to those He loves."

I opened my eyes to something wet, brushing my nose and saw Luna, my son's Australian shepherd, by my bedside. I remembered I had a dream, so I deduce I did eventually fall asleep after I prayed.

Sleepless nights were frequent occurrences during my menopausal years and times when I felt anxious and over-exhausted.

Adequate, quality sleep helps our body to perform optimally. Sleep affects multiple bodily functions. According to the National Heart, Lung, and Blood Institute, a good night's rest influences how our brain works, improves learning, enhances our problem-solving skills, supports healthy growth and development, keeps our immune system functioning, and maintains a healthy balance of hormones responsible for weight management. Healing and repair of our heart and blood vessels occur while we are asleep. A lack of sleep affects our decision-making, the control of our emotions and behavior, and how we cope with change.[37]

Early morning awakenings disturbed my sleep too, so I sought my doctor's help. He referred me to the Sleep Clinic. The staff at the clinic taught me how to use Cognitive Behavioral Therapy (CBT) or Sleep Therapy to change my sleep pattern. First, I had to identify the most suitable time for me to go to sleep. Using a process they directed me to perform for several nights, I discovered that when I was in bed by ten, I fell asleep faster. Going to bed later than that time, made falling asleep a challenge. They also taught me to change my negative thoughts and beliefs to positive ones and to relax before bed. I identified habits that kept me from having a good night's rest and changed them. I stopped watching the news before I went to bed and made sure my phone was turned off. When I went past my bedtime, I applied lavender lotion and found that helped me. I also drank caffeine-free Chamomile tea before bed.

Chewing Gum

Driving alone in the car caused additional stress because of the richness of my imagination. Anxious thoughts kept derailing my peace of mind. I found chewing gum to be helpful. The constant mastication distracted me from unruly thoughts. The peppermint flavor induced belching which released the build-up of gas in my abdominal cavity which commonly occurs when I am stressed. This eased the tightness in my chest allowing me to breathe easier and kept me from pursuing a rabbit trail of worry.

Being our own advocate, partnering with our health care professional

My blood pressure was stable after being on medication for years and my doctor recommended that I stop taking it. Aware that I was taking a beta blocker, a drug that not only reduced blood pressure but also slowed the heart rate and diminished irregular heart rhythms, I requested to continue taking them to keep my heart rate regulated. He conceded. Continuing my treatment hand-in-hand with a professional while making sure I was mindful of my diet and exercising gives me a sense of control. We are the first champions of our health. Having a good working relationship and communication with our physician is a must.

Balanced—Busy but not exhausted

I gained my fondness for reading and listening to people telling stories in elementary school. Every Wednesday, I searched for treasures, I submerged in waters with sunken ships or traveled to exotic places as our librarian kept my mind captive in the tales she read to us. Stories about "Juan Tamad" stand out to me. *Tamad* in the vernacular means lazy. These folktales featuring the main character, Juan, offered a moral lesson, yet they were comedic.

True to his nickname, Juan was a lazy fellow. His laziness was evident in the story about a guava. Juan fancied eating a fruit from the guava tree. He laid down under the tree and waited for the fruit to fall so he could eat it. In another narrative, Juan's mom asked him to buy crabs from the local market. Juan went to the market and purchased the live crabs as directed. Walking home under the intensity of the midday sun, Juan grew tired. He came across a tree and took a nap under its shade. He knew his mom wanted to serve the crabs for lunch. So, before he slumbered, he untied the cords that bundled the crabs together and instructed them to walk home, giving them directions on how to get there. The crustaceans did not end up on their lunch menu.

Juan's stories remind us what Proverbs 19:24 says, "The sluggard buries his hand in the dish and will not even bring it back to his mouth." Ecclesiastes 10:18 points out that, "Through laziness, the rafters sag; because of idle hands, the house leaks." Ecclesiastes 11:6 states, "Sow your seed in the morning, and at evening let your hands not be idle for you do not know which will succeed, whether this or that, or whether both will do equally well." All these verses imply how laziness and idleness could be to our detriment.

Since my parents were civil servants in their careers, I learned the value of work and producing something with my hands. Boredom was not part of my vocabulary. I engaged in many activities—climbing trees, wading in a nature-made pool after a massive deluge, spending time with friends, or walking around my block. Idleness was not my thing.

As an adult, I was at the radical end of the continuum. I became too busy. I was the mother of two young children, I worked full-time as a teacher, had a small business, and volunteered in the women's ministry at church.

It was hard for me to say "no" and I became a "Jacquette-of-all-trades." As a "yes" lady, I took on and juggled people's requests. I felt they needed me, and I desired to do, do, do. The stacked schedule and my choices did not decrease my anxiousness nor lend to a peaceful me. No wonder I ended up exhausted most days.

Though being lazy and idle is not desirable, overcommitment is not idyllic either. Idleness gives room for negative thoughts **Balance is key.** to consume our minds; thoughts that lead us to experience our Fear Giants and allow our jungles to creep in. Staying busy keeps our mind off our anxious thoughts. However, when we tip the scales and overdo things, we also open the door for stress to join us—with additional stress, more anxiety.

The story of creation illustrates how much we require rest. God created the heavens and the earth and everything in it in six days, and then He rested on the seventh day. He modeled the importance of rest. In Psalm 46:10, He reminds us to be still and know that He is God.

Balance is key.

• • •

Eliminating what won't help—our pest and weed protocols

As we add fertilizers to enhance growth of plants, we can likewise use good pest and weed management techniques to reduce the growth of weeds and propagation of pests. Healthy pest and weed controls stand for things we can eliminate from our daily routines and keep our jungle of fear symptoms from developing. Good pest management helps promote healthy crops.

Starving our Fears

Along with orchids, Sal and I grow succulents. Neither succulents nor orchids like to be overwatered. I water them only once a week, making sure they drain well, too. Our succulents and orchids are all over the house. Once, I put one of our more beautiful succulents by the window in our formal dining room, a room we hardly used. The saying "Out of sight, out of mind," proved true in this situation. I completely forgot to water that succulent, and sure enough, it died. This principle is also true with our jungle.

If we do not feed the negative thoughts in our mind, we are breaking the vicious cycle of fear-jungle-more fear-uncontrollable jungle. When we allow our minds to spin with the vortex of gloom and doom, there is no room for the good that comes from God. Romans 12:2 says, "Do not conform to the pattern of this world, but be transformed by the renewing of your mind. Then you will be able to test and approve what God's will is—his good, pleasing, and perfect will." God has a perfect plan for us, and it is good and pleasing. So how do we empty our thoughts of the negative? Like a magnet that has polar opposites, we think of the positive.

Philippians 4:8 states, "Finally, brothers and sisters, whatever is true, whatever is noble, whatever is right, whatever is pure, whatever is lovely, whatever is admirable—is excellent or praiseworthy--think about such things." To aid me in remembering this verse, I put together the acronym, TENLAPPR. This acronym stands for each of the things I need to keep my mind on, that which is **t**rue, **e**xcellent, **n**oble, **l**ovely, **a**dmirable, **p**raiseworthy, **p**ure, and **r**ight. Changing our focus will not come naturally. Asking the Holy Spirit to help us is necessary. He is the one Jesus has given to empower us. We starve our negative thoughts by replacing them with positive ones with the tenacity of an athlete disciplining his body and mind to achieve his goal.

Smoking Our Worries Away

"Why do you fan smoke to the mango trees, *Nanay*?" I asked my grandmother during one of my visits to her. Every afternoon my grandma used to sweep fallen leaves and branches, gather them into a pile, and burn them. The final piece of this ritual was to fan the smoke toward the mango trees if the wind did not blow it to their direction.

"So they will have more flowers and more fruit," she responded.

True enough, we used to enjoy an abundance of this tropical fruit. As I grew older, I learned that this was a natural method used in the Philippines to help mangoes flower and produce fruits. Smoke also prevented fruit flies from attacking and drove mosquitoes away.

"Poof!"

The words on pieces of paper disappeared in the smoke. This was my regular morning routine at our kitchen sink. I wrote anything and everything that worried me and after I prayed and gave each worry to the Lord, I burned each piece of paper, symbolizing my releasing them into His loving hands. As using smoke helped increase the abundance of flowers on mango trees, this symbolic gesture of burning my worries into smoke is one concrete act of my surrendering them to the Lord, thus allowing more blossoms of peace to grow. What can you symbolically do as a gesture of letting go of your worries?

Giving up our cup of Joe and minding our sugar

I have always had a faster heart rate than average for a person my age. When symptoms of fear manifest, it increases it even more. Knowing that drinking coffee can escalate my heart rate, I opt for decaffeinated drinks.

I have felt the ill effect of caffeine on my heart on a few different occasions.

We hosted a high school student from Thailand for ten months. At the end of the tenth month, we took her to where her group was assembling to be debriefed. They were preparing them for their departure back to their country of origin. While waiting for everyone to arrive, Sal asked me to get coffee from Starbucks. I ordered three, one for Sal, one for her, and one for me. Both hers and Sal's Frappuccinos were regular caffeinated drinks while I ordered the White Mocha Frappuccino decaf for myself. Unfortunately, I mistakenly gave Sal my drink and I had his. I suffered the rapid drum-like beating in my chest for two days.

The second incident occurred when Sal and I attended a timeshare presentation in Las Vegas. The salesperson stopped in the middle of his spiel, and asked me, "Are you OK, Mrs. Valoria?"

"I'm good," I replied, "why?"

"You seem jittery."

This surprised me. Back in our hotel room, I pondered on what made him say what he did. Then I realized something. I had been popping cough drops one after another to relieve the soreness in my throat. Since the cough drops were packaged in candy form,

I did not think much of potential side effects. Candy cough drops contain sugar that can contribute to an increase in our blood sugar level. This explained the jitteriness I was experiencing. In an interview with Healthline, Erin Palinski-Wade, M.D., a nutrition and diet expert, speaker and author of several books on diabetes states, "Added sugars cause your blood sugar to go on a roller coaster ride of spikes and crashes and with it, your energy also goes up and down. When blood sugar crashes, your mood sours and anxiety levels can spike."[38]

Green tea, highly recommended for its health benefit, was my choice of beverage at least two or three times a day. What I did not realize was that green tea contained caffeine no matter how relatively small it was. Unknowingly, the caffeine and sugar I was consuming compounded my anxiety.

After this discovery, I attempted to limit my use of lozenges and my intake of green tea. I now choose caffeine-free herbal teas to take its place. I have also resorted to preparing myself for the cold and cough seasons by using or consuming natural homemade remedies and resources or sources, such as pineapple which is high in Vitamin C. Having made these changes, I seem to be more immune to colds and coughs.

• • •

Being rooted and connected in Him, remembering His faithfulness, waiting on Him, enhancing the soil of my mind and body, eliminating those things that do not promote peace in our lives are ways that help us persevere.

Part 4

Acquiring Maintenance

"Efficiency is a great secret
that can drop us right into our ideal life path,
but it is a hard one to practice and
something that takes constant
maintenance and work."

—Tara Stiles

CHAPTER 14

Drought Resistant, Drought Tolerant, Drought Avoidance

At the beginning of the school year, our Garden Club started with seven fourth through sixth graders. As time went by, it dwindled. Five. Four. Three. One.

I couldn't discredit my ten-to-eleven-year-olds for their abandonment. Waking up early to be at school at 7:45 a.m. once a week can be tough. What made it even more difficult was a few of them had multiple extracurricular activities they were involved with while keeping up with a rigorous curriculum. With the change in our meetings from Friday to Tuesday mornings and a particularly rainy winter, we could not maintain a consistent schedule.

Fortunately, we prepped all the planter boxes and planted the bulbs early in the year. By mid-spring the garden was looking like a jungle again with the rain encouraging not only the beautiful lily blooms but also the weeds to tower over.

One.
That was me.

I had to keep on weeding by myself. It seemed the weeds had the upper hand, but the fighter in me did not want to give up. I was at the helm of keeping our garden looking beautiful, so responsible I had better be!

The sun's rays replaced the pit-pattering rain. A smile appeared on my lips. Short-lived, though, as I contended with the unpredictability of our climate. With the blink of an eye, the long, dry, stretch of summer faced us.

Then another problem appeared. The metal spigot that controlled the water system in the garden rusted and when Sal turned it on, it broke. No water was available for our planter boxes. The abundant spring rain was gone and my main water source for the summer was unavailable. It is easy to say, "you just need to replace the spigot," but when you have a limited amount of time, it is difficult. I had to figure out how to get water to our plants, to make sure the intense heat of the sun did not send them to an early grave. I knew I had to prepare for the drought.

This same scenario happens in our fight against our anxieties and fears. As it is necessary to prepare for the drought to affect the garden in our school, we also need to be ready for times of drought in our fight against our Fear Giants. Sometimes we have a great crowd of supporters and encouragers, but there are moments when it seems we are lone rangers. We rummage through our contact list and find no one available. Everyone has somewhere to go to or is distracted by something. Though our loved ones intend to be there for us, life happens. We get busy. They get busy.

We feel loneliness and hopelessness approach. We experience relational drought.

We need to be ready for these times. Times when the going gets tough or tougher.

Moments when we feel no one is there for us. Weeks when we see no change, and everything seem broken. Periods when stressors steadily erupt in our lives, and it seems our prayers hit the ceiling and stay there—a spiritual drought.

These are moments we must summon back memories of victorious times—we

We need to prepare for relational and spiritual droughts.

dust our slings and polish our five stones. We need to stretch our perseverance muscles so we can get to the finish line, victorious. We cannot throw in the towel. We need to protect ourselves and continue to be advocates for our healing.

To keep our garden of peace thriving, we need to be drought resistant, drought tolerant and by all means, avoid the drought. We need to keep our tools on hand.

Every now and then I wake up in the middle of the night or early dawn with my heart pounding. In the darkness of my bedroom, my thoughts wander through a labyrinth of irrationality. My mind goes haywire. I question if my adult children are in places where they could get hurt, or if my relatives on the other side of the world are in crisis. I deal with all the "what if's" my mind can conjure.

Aroused from my sleep, I switch on my reading light. I grab my Bible. I flip through its pages to take hold of my sword—the sword of the Spirit, which is the Word of God.

Then I claim it.

My favorite go-to in times like this is Psalm 121 which I have put to memory. "I lift up my eyes to the mountains—where does my help come from? My help comes from the Lord, the Maker of heaven and earth. He will not let your foot slip—He who watches over you will not slumber; indeed, He who watches over Israel will neither slumber nor sleep. The Lord watches over you—the Lord is your shade at your right hand; the sun will not harm you by day, nor the moon by night. The Lord will keep you from all harm—He will watch over your life; the Lord will watch over your coming and going both now and forevermore."

I pray and declare this for whoever I worry about, including myself. Doing this puts my mind to rest and at ease. Like smoke from the burnt pieces of paper in front of my sink, my worries and fears dissipate into thin air.

With Psalm 121 on my mind, I am lulled back to sleep secure that the God who controls the universe is watching over my loved ones and me.

Ready for Battle

With my daily maintenance medication, I do my daily meditation.

Waking up at 5:00 in the morning and doing my devotion on God's Word and praying keeps my mind and body ready for whatever I may encounter throughout my day.

I start by asking the Holy Spirit to guide me and give me discernment. Then I study His Word. I do this by focusing on a particular Bible verse or verses, or studying a whole passage of Scripture. As I gain insights into His Word, I jot them down and include how I can apply them in my life. I also journal my prayer requests and answered prayers. Journaling helped me when I was a new believer. During those earlier days, my mind would go on rabbit trails while I prayed. I would start saying something then my thoughts would go off on a tangent. Journaling helped me to retrain my brain to stay focused. After I write in my journal, I pray.

So, what is prayer and how do we pray?

Prayer is communicating with God. Communication is a two-way street. Effective

We need to give God a chance to talk to us.

communication happens when we listen to each other and give each other a chance to talk. I love to talk, so I have to remind myself that I have two ears to listen and one mouth to speak. We need to give God a chance to talk to us. Psalm 46:10 tells us, "He says, 'Be still, and know that I am God; I will be exalted among the nations, I will be exalted in the earth.'"

Using the acronym ACTS also aided in keeping my prayers focused.

Adoration

Confession

Thanksgiving

Supplication

This acronym gives us the four elements of prayer and arranges it in the order of importance.[39]

We acknowledge who God is first, above all else. He deserves it and is worthy of this place.

Daily we face battles on many fronts. We battle against our Fear Giants. We battle against the pressures and demands of this world to stay on top of things, to be ahead of our game, to provide for our family's needs. We battle against our desires and the mores of society. Scripture says our fiercest battle is not against flesh and blood but against principalities, against forces that we cannot see (Ephesians 6:10–13).

Jesus faced similar enticements when Satan tried to tempt Him in the wilderness. With every attempt, Jesus crushed them down by quoting His Father's Word (Matthew 4:1–11).

To culminate my prayer time, I do as Ephesians 6:14–17 tells me, "Stand firm then, with the belt of truth buckled around your waist, with the breastplate of righteousness in place, and with your feet fitted with the readiness that comes from the gospel of peace. In addition to all this, take up the shield of faith, with which you can extinguish all the flaming arrows of the evil one. Take the helmet of salvation and the sword of the Spirit, which is the word of God."

So how do we do this?

Mentally and spiritually we visualize donning on every part of God's armor. We do this on behalf of ourselves and our family.

Tightly grasping the sword of the Spirit with our right hand we get ourselves ready to strike any attempts the enemy has to destroy us. Holding the shield of faith in God's love, goodness, and power, we protect ourselves from the flaming arrows of worries, doubts, and fears. We ward off concerns of the future with His helmet of salvation, reminding us He has our future in the palm of His hands.

Mentally and spiritually we visualize donning on every part of God's armor.

We dismiss the enemies' lies as we gird our loins with God's belt of truth. Truths of our identity as children of God standing in the blessings of being His (John 1:12). Trusting in the verity that we can stand firm in His Word and can receive His peace which surpasses all understanding as we cling to Him (Philippians 4:7). We listen to the Holy Spirit whispering in our ears the truth that we are safe in God's loving arms when our Fear Giants attempt a chokehold on us (Deuteronomy 12:10). The truth that wherever we are, He is with us (Joshua 1:9).

Then we put on His breastplate of righteousness. The righteousness that took us from being condemned to redeemed (Ephesians 1:7). No longer do we need to feel guilt or shame for we have been made clean and our relationship with Him is restored. Free from the bondage of sin, we are emancipated from the prison of needing to please people. Our freedom allows God to shape us into the person He wants us to be.

Our armor is incomplete, so we put on the final piece—we slip on the sandals of the gospel of peace. We stand on the hope of Jesus and what He did on the cross. Peace, that even amid difficulties and struggles, will sustain us. As we do this, we can stand firm and not fear, for He promised He goes with us and will never leave us nor forsake us (Deuteronomy 31:6).

Like medication taken daily, this is our spiritual and relational maintenance dose. His Word protects and shelters us. We keep our sling by our side and our stones on hand. When we do this daily, it keeps us fully dressed and ready for battle. It covers us from the top of our heads to the tip of our toes, and the enemy cannot penetrate. We become drought resistant, drought tolerant, and drought avoidant.

And we can raise our hands in praise and thanksgiving to our God who proclaims, "I have told you these things, so that in me you may have peace. In this world you will have trouble. But take heart! I have overcome the world" (John 16:33).

EPILOGUE

As the driver pulled over and parked my cousin's SUV in an already crowded unpaved lot, I got a clearer view of the pristine picture in front of us. Framed with coconut trees on the sides, the sandy beach in front of me opened to the blue, calm, sprawling waters of the Pacific Ocean. The aromatic smell of sea salt awakened my senses even more this early morning. The sun shone brightly. It was warm, but my hands were a little cold and shaky. I felt the moistness as the humid air brushed my skin. My heart thumped extra beats here and there.

I was both apprehensive and excited for this adventure. I thought Sal and I would do it together, only to find out he changed his mind at the last minute. I was confronted with going alone—taking an outrigger canoe with two strangers to the middle of the ocean and then swimming with gigantic creatures with big mouths and spotted skins—whale sharks. Not just one but most likely five or six of them. I wanted to back out too. But we were already there. We had travelled via a roll-on roll-off ferry from Dumaguete City to the southern tip of the neighboring island of Cebu and then drove for three hours to get to this place. It was not the time to retreat.

I checked my options with the lady at the information booth. There were two. At a lower price, I could just sit in the canoe and peer into the water down below and get a glimpse of the swimming giants. The second was to get into the water and experience this once in a lifetime adventure. The first choice appealed to me. It was the safer one, the selection that did not put me in the unknown of what was lurking underneath the outrigger canoe.

But something in me clamored for that adventure. I begged Sal to reconsider. He did not relent. Sal and the lapping waves did not agree.

Despite the uncertainty, I decided.

I would do it.

Clad in my swimsuit and an orange life vest, I held on to the goggles and snorkel with my right hand as I took awkward steps toward the canoe and waved to Sal taking my picture; *Oh well, that might be the last.*

Looking around me and quietly reciting Psalm 121, I reassured myself. There were other canoes at a distance, some with little kids. *No matter what happens, God is with me.*

After some distance, the two guys manning the canoe stopped paddling. One of them lowered himself into the water. In its clarity, I could tell the water was deep. I could swim but I wasn't that strong of a swimmer. The other man reminded me not to make any splashing noises as he instructed me to put my goggles and snorkel on. I told him to wait as he stretched out his hand to assist me onto the side of the outrigger. I took a moment to take in what I was about to do. My mind raised with opposing choices. *Stay on the canoe, get into the water. Stay on the canoe, get into the water.*

With utmost care, I lowered myself. I could feel the pressure on my knuckles as I clung onto the rafter.

The man on the canoe told me to let go and swim. With my left hand continuing to hold on, I let my right arm go, and slipped into the water. In the corner of my eye, I saw something big pass by. *Could that be it?*

The guy who was in the water moved closer to where I was. He pointed to where the whale sharks were and encouraged me to swim. I released my grip from the rafter and propelled myself farther away from the canoe. One after another, as if on cue, whale sharks glided effortlessly close to where I was. I realized I was swimming amidst six of them. I had conquered my fear!

We have two choices in our struggle with our Fear Giants and jungles. One, we could sit and watch them wreak havoc in our lives. The second option would be to dive in deep, understand and deal with them, knowing that we are not alone; there is help and hope. The Fear Giants may wage their war against my peace, but every time God shows me His faithfulness in dealing with them, my roots of belief grow deeper and I can stand firm.

To this day I continue to experience rapid heart rates and a rush of irrational thoughts every now and then when confronted by situations that take me out of my comfort zone. As a Christian, I used to feel guilty that I had these symptoms. *Shouldn't I have Christ's peace in me every moment of the day since He is in me? Is my faith weak?* Then just as fast as all these doubts and questions creep in, God's Word ushers them out. John 16:33 says, "I have told you these things, so that in me you may have peace. In this world you will have trouble. But take heart! I have overcome the world."

Then I kick myself back into gear understanding that I am still in this broken world and with all the human frailties. As long as we are alive in this world, we will experience fears, worry, and anxiety. But take heart, we have God's promise that He has overcome the world, and because we have Him, we too have the victory. God can use these times as opportunities for us to be safe and to develop our trust in Him.

Now and then, I revisit the little girl approaching the piano bench, choked up in all her fears, and in her place, I see a woman who might still have fears but now has faith and hope. Hope that emanates from the One who made her. Hope that can slay any Fear Giant that threatens to pounce on her. Hope that allows beautiful gardens of peace to grow. A woman who understands and accepts who she was and is. One who can take her sling and either with one, two, three, four, or five stones, slay her Fear Giants. One who allows the Lord to let her garden grow and blossom.

So, my challenge to you is this, if you haven't given your life to the Lord, try Him. He promises in John 6:37, "All those the Father gives me will come to me, and whoever comes to me I will never drive away." Accept who you are and what you feel. Equip yourself with His Word and the power of His Holy Spirit. Draw warmth from His perfect love. Bask in His goodness and faithfulness through worship in your songs of praise and thanksgiving. Sharpen your vision as you take His perspective. Stand strong believing in your prayer. Finish well persevering through the tough times.

Go slay your Fear Giants and cut down those jungles.

Then grow those gardens and as the saying by Saint Francis de Sales, Bishop of Geneva (1567-1622) goes, "bloom where you are planted."[40]

But blessed is the man who trusts in the Lord, whose con-
fidence is in Him. He will be like a tree planted by water
that sends out is roots by the stream. It does not fear when
heat comes; its leaves are always green. It has no worries
in a year of drought and never fails to bear fruit.

Jeremiah 17:7-8 NIV

ACKNOWLEDGEMENTS

To my prayer supporters and partners, sisters in Christ, and BFF's—Ingrid Pil-Vasquez, Bambi Gayotin, Sylvia Corona, Gail Hibbs, Janette Delaney, Jennifer Steele, and the many others who have been recipients of my countless prayer requests, thank you for standing in the gap for me.

To my beta readers, Wendy Kaschak, Bambi Gayotin, and Ruth Gelbond, your valuable input is very much appreciated.

To Kary Oberbrunner, David Branderhorst, Nanette O'Neal, Abigail Young, Niccie Kliegl, Brenda Haire, Tanisha Williams, Erica Foster, and the entire AAE team and the Igniting Souls Tribe, thank you for your coaching, support, encouragement, and guidance.

To the Inspire Christian Writers Group and my writing critique team under the leadership of Dana Sudboro—Ruth Morse, John Kaschak, Ricky Charlet, Frieda Yang, Florentine Pfluger, James Burgess, Larry Mandelberg, and Beth Perry, thank you for encouraging and helping me hone my skills to become a better writer.

To Lysa TerKeurst, Suzie Eller, Glynnis Whitwer, Karen Ehman, Heather Holleman, the Compel Training Team, and the Proverbs 31 ministry, thank you for providing women with great resources, teaching, inspiration, and encouragement to help us not only to be the writers God wants us to become but to also live our lives for His glory and honor.

To Luke Hibbs, you are a blessed photographer! Thank you for making my photo shoot fun.

To my parents, Antonio and Cecilia Alamo and my siblings, Antonio Alamo, Jr., Violeta Alamo (nee Dasal), Waldemar Alamo, and the Bartolo and Alamo clan, and my aunt, Charito Lopez. Your nurturing and unquestioning support, faith, and love have allowed me to grow up to pursue my potential and my dreams.

To my spiritual parents, Cory and Danilo Varela, thank you for your obedience to our Savior. You showed me the way to the Lord and for that I am forever grateful. To Pastor Nasali Silava and Campus Crusade for Christ, thank you for your ministry which God has used and continues to use to lead people to Him.

To my VIVA '77 family, I am so blessed by all of you and I treasure our friendship.

To my classmates Joel Gamo, M.D., Mark Lauron, M.D., and Mark Operario, M.D., thank you for your invaluable input.

To my children, Camille and Christian, and son-in-love, Chris, your prayers, unconditional love, passion and love for the Lord and support continue to inspire me and keep me encouraged in my own walk with Him.

To my husband, Sal, I cannot thank God enough for blessing me with you. You have been my supporter through my crazy ideas all these years.

NOTES

Chapter 1

1 Quotes.net, STANDS4 LLC, 2019. **"The Godfather: Part II Quotes."** Accessed September 22, 2019. https://www.quotes.net/mquote/1093422.

2 "Who Said, 'Keep Your Friends Close and Your Enemies Closer?'." *Quora*, www.quora.com/Who-said-Keep-your-friends-close-and-your-enemies-closer.

3 "Jungle." Wikipedia. Wikimedia Foundation, September 21, 2019. https://en.wikipedia.org/wiki/Jungle.

Chapter 2

4 Pearson, Steve. "What Happened in 1960 Important News and Events, Key Technology and Popular Culture." The People History. Accessed September 22, 2019. http://www.thepeoplehistory.com/1960.html.

5 Walsh, Jeffrey. "Emotions: Limbic System." Khan Academy. Khan Academy. Accessed September 22, 2019. https://www.khanacademy.org/science/health-and-medicine/executive-systems-of-the-brain/emotion-lesson/v/emotions-limbic-system.

6 Walsh, Jeffrey. "Emotions: Limbic System." Khan Academy. Khan Academy. Accessed September 22, 2019. https://www.khanacademy.org/science/

health-and-medicine/executive-systems-of-the-brain/
emotion-lesson/v/emotions-limbic-system.

7 Harvard Health Publishing. "Understanding
the Stress Response." *Harvard Health*, 2018,
www.health.harvard.edu/staying-healthy/
understanding-the-stress-response.

8 "Adrenaline & Cortisol." *LIVESTRONG.
COM*, Leaf Group, www.livestrong.com/articl
e/207432-adrenaline-cortisol/.

9 Walsh, Jeffrey. "Emotions: Limbic System." Khan
Academy. Khan Academy. Accessed September
22, 2019. https://www.khanacademy.org/science/
health-and-medicine/executive-systems-of-the-brain/
emotion-lesson/v/emotions-limbic-system.

10 Walsh, Jeffrey. "Emotions: Limbic System." Khan
Academy. Khan Academy. Accessed September
22, 2019. https://www.khanacademy.org/science/
health-and-medicine/executive-systems-of-the-brain/
emotion-lesson/v/emotions-limbic-system.

Chapter 4

11 "Anirudh." Learnodo Newtonic, September 14,
2018. https://www.learnodo-newtonic.com/
georgia-okeeffe-facts.

12 "Georgia O'Keeffe Quotes." BrainyQuote. Xplore.
Accessed September 19, 2019. https://www.
brainyquote.com/authors/georgia-okeeffe-quotes.

13 "Lao Tzu Quotes (Author of Tao Te Ching)."
Goodreads. Goodreads, n.d. https://www.goodreads.
com/author/quotes/2622245.Lao_Tzu.

Chapter 5

[14] "Elah Valley (BiblePlaces.com)." BiblePlaces.
com. Accessed September 19, 2019. https://www.
bibleplaces.com/elahvalley/.

[15] "Sling (Weapon)." Wikipedia. Wikimedia Foundation,
August 3, 2019. https://en.wikipedia.org/wiki/Sling_
(weapon).

Chapter 8

[16] Ho, Leon. "How Long Does It Take to Break a
Habit? Science Will Tell You." Lifehack. Lifehack,
February 19, 2019. https://www.lifehack.org/667495/
how-long-does-it-take-to-break-a-habit.

Chapter 9

[17] "Martin Luther King, Jr. Quotes." BrainyQuote.
Xplore. Accessed September 19, 2019. https://
www.brainyquote.com/quotes/martin_luther_king_
jr_101472.

Chapter 10

[18] "Viewpoint." Merriam-Webster. Merriam-Webster.
Accessed September 19, 2019. https://www.
merriam-webster.com/dictionary/viewpoint.

[19] "Perspective." Merriam-Webster. Merriam-Webster.
Accessed September 19, 2019. https://www.
merriam-webster.com/dictionary/perspective.

[20] Masoner, Liz. "How to Use Point of View to Improve
Your Photos." The Spruce Crafts. The Spruce Crafts,
May 29, 2019. https://www.thesprucecrafts.com/
explanation-of-point-of-view-photography-4072926.

21 "Dolly Parton Quotes." BrainyQuote. Xplore. Accessed September 19, 2019. https://www.brainyquote.com/ quotes/dolly_parton_126881.

Chapter 11

22 "Praise." *Merriam-Webster*, Merriam-Webster, www. merriam-webster.com/dictionary/praise.
23 "Worship." *Merriam-Webster*, Merriam-Webster, www. merriam-webster.com/dictionary/worship.
24 "Thanksgiving." *Merriam-Webster*, Merriam-Webster, www.merriam-webster.com/dictionary/thanksgiving.
25 "Hallowed." *Merriam-Webster*. Merriam-Webster. Accessed September 19, 2019. https://www. merriam-webster.com/dictionary/hallowed.
26 CBS News. "How Mozart's Music Is Improving the Grapes in One Italian Vineyard." CBS News. CBS Interactive, January 2, 2017. https://www.cbsnews. com/news/mozart-classical-music-helps-grapes-gro w-italy-vineyard/.
27 "Music Therapy and Mental Health." Accessed 2019. https://www.musictherapy.org/assets/1/7/MT_ Mental_Health_2006.pdf.
28 "Neurologic Music Therapy." cammomusic. org. Accessed September 23, 2019. http://www. cammomusic.org/cammo-offers/music-therapy/ what-is-music-therapy.

Chapter 12

29 Laffargue, Charles-André. "Ferdinand Foch." *Encyclopædia Britannica*, Encyclopædia Britannica, Inc., www.britannica.com/biography/Ferdinand-Foch.

30   "Passion." Merriam-Webster. Merriam-Webster. Accessed September 29, 2019. https://www. merriam-webster.com/dictionary/passion.

Chapter 13

31   "How to Water Succulent Plants." *Succulents and Sunshine*, 4 May 2019, www.succulentsandsunshine. com/how-to-water-succulent-plants/.

32   "Top 10 Ralph Waldo Emerson Quotes." BrainyQuote. Xplore. Accessed September 20, 2019. https://www.brainyquote.com/lists/authors/ top-10-ralph-waldo-emerson-quotes.

33   "Open-and-Go Lessons That Inspire Kids to Love Science." Mystery Science. Accessed September 20, 2019. https://mysteryscience.com/ecosystems/ ecosystems-the-food-web.

34   "Deep Breathing Exercises & Techniques for Stress Management and Relief." *WebMD*, WebMD, www.webmd.com/balance/stress-management/ stress-relief-breathing-techniques#1.

35   Helmenstine, Anne Marie. "How Much of the Human Body Is Water?" ThoughtCo. ThoughtCo, May 13, 2019. https://www.thoughtco.com/ how-much-of-your-body-is-water-609406.

36   "Banana Natural Beta Blocker for Anxiety." *Health Extremist*, 2 Apr. 2019, www.healthextremist.com/ banana-a-natural-beta-blocker-for-anxiety/.

37   "Sleep Deprivation and Deficiency." *National Heart Lung and Blood Institute*, U.S. Department of Health and Human Services, www.nhlbi.nih.gov/ health-topics/sleep-deprivation-and-deficiency.

38   "The 5 Worst Foods for Your Anxiety." *Healthline*, Healthline Media, www.healthline.com/health/ mental-health/surprising-foods-trigger-anxiety#6.

Chapter 14

[39] Sproul, R.C. "A Simple Acrostic for Prayer: A.C.T.S." *Ligonier Ministries*, www.ligonier.org/blog/simple-acrostic-prayer/.

Epilogue

[40] "Bloom Where You Are Planted." Just Pieces..., January 4, 2010. https://tomlangford.wordpress.com/2010/01/03/bloom-where-youre-planted/.

ABOUT THE AUTHOR

Cecille Valoria is an elementary school teacher, author, speaker, and coach. Having struggled with anxiety early on in her life, her mission is to bring hope to people who struggle with fears and excessive worry. Though her background in Psychology and Medicine have come in handy in understanding this challenge, she attributes her peace and healing from her relationship with the Lord. She has built her community around the belief that "true friendships don't fade away, they linger forever." She lives in Sacramento, CA. with her husband. They have two kids and a son-in-love. Cecille loves traveling, photography, and flowers and is the founder of Flowers for Elders, an organization that delivers flower arrangements to patients. You can connect with her at CecilleValoria.com

Everyone has a story to tell.

Are you ready to write yours?

**Author Academy Elite can help
you write, publish, and
market your book.**

Learn more at:

http://bit.ly/GotaStory

"You can't experience true success or significance if you don't know WHO you are and WHOSE you are. To make an impact upon the world you must understand what it means to be connected to your Creator, CORE, and community." -**Kary Oberbrunner, Author, Your Secret Name**

Don't go through another day without knowing who you were created to be

Join me through this 5-week interactive course to self-discovery.

Your Secret Name 5 Week Journey is a step-by-step process to make this desire your reality.

This 100% online learning experience is right for you if:

- You desire to reset your self-image set-point.
- You want to become who you were born to be.
- You are tired of wearing a mask and suffering from imposter syndrome.
- You want to be set free from your past and live in light of a new future.
- You would benefit from deeper and richer relationship with yourself, others people, and the God who made you.
- You're ready to live according to the way God sees you and not the way others do.

Connect with me at <u>CecilleValoria.com</u> today to get you started on this journey.